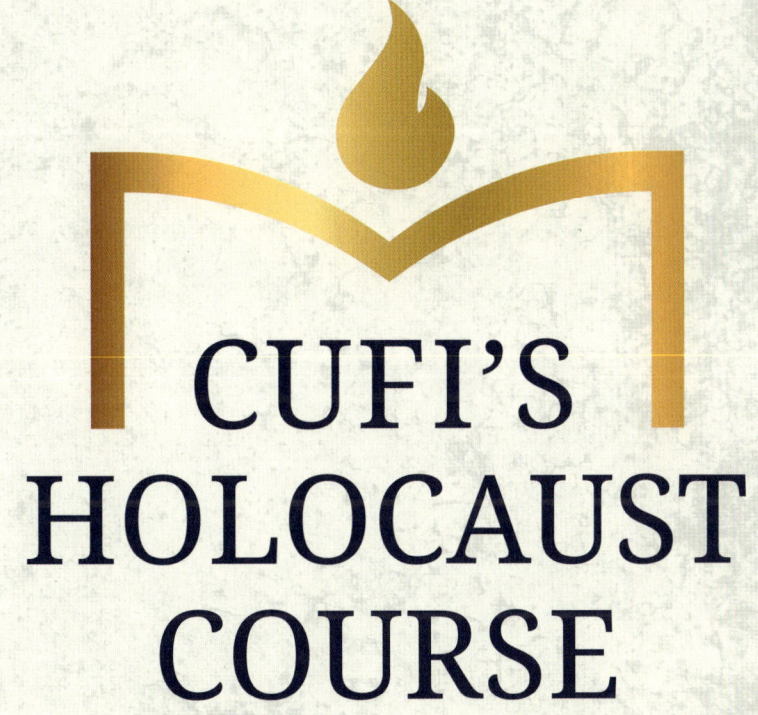

CUFI'S HOLOCAUST COURSE

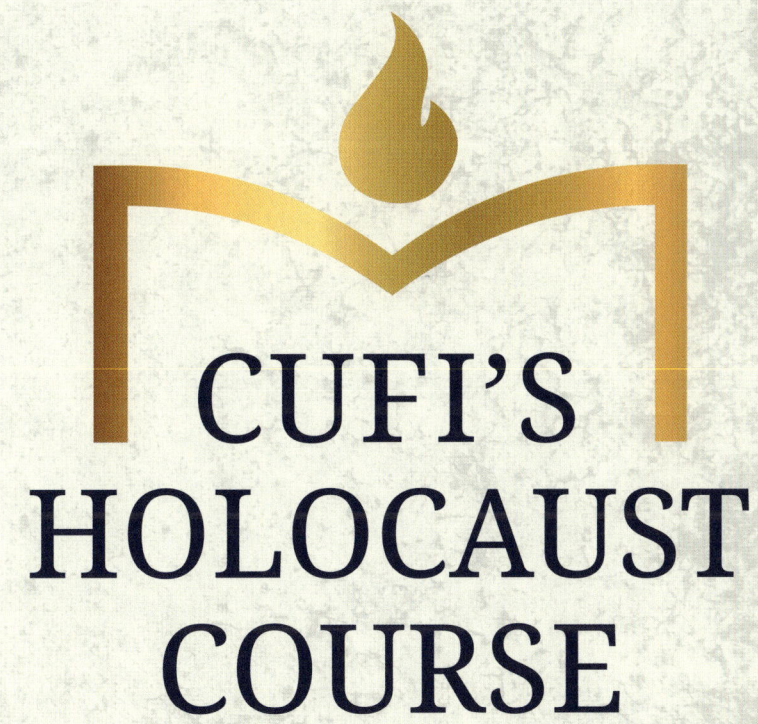

CUFI'S HOLOCAUST COURSE

TABLE OF CONTENTS

INTRODUCTION

The Holocaust is the genocide by which all others are measured. After more than a millennium of European antisemitism, Adolf Hitler found a sympathetic ear for his Jew-hatred among many throughout the continent. His effort to obliterate the existence of the Jewish people began not long after he took the position of Chancellor in 1933.

In 1935, only two years into Hitler's role as Chancellor, the Nuremberg Laws were enacted, stripping Jews of both basic human and civil rights. Three years later, in 1938, the pogrom known as *Kristallnacht* (The Night of Broken Glass) struck a marked escalation in violence against Jews — with thousands of Jewish-owned businesses, synagogues, and homes destroyed, and over 30,000 Jewish men sent to concentration camps. It was on this horrific night that the Nazis first engaged in a mass roundup and deportation of Jews. Hitler's "Final Solution" to the "Jewish problem" graduated from largely economic, political, and social marginalization to direct violence against Jews.

Between 1941 and 1945, through the powerful Nazi war machine, the systematic extermination of six million Jewish men, women, and children across Europe was orchestrated. For the Jewish people, it was a time when pure evil reigned with no apparent end in sight.

The Nazis' atrocities against their Jewish victims were industrial in their scale. They engaged in grotesque human scientific experiments and murdered the weak. The able-bodied were enslaved, until they were exterminated. Two-thirds of the European Jewish population was murdered during the Holocaust.

In 1939, there were 16.6 million members of the Jewish faith in the world. Almost ninety years later, there are presently 15.8 million Jews in the world today. Hitler's atrocities, and the centuries of antisemitism that enabled them, changed the world forever, and the Jewish population has yet to recover.

And yet, even against the backdrop of these atrocities, there emerged profound stories of courage, resilience, and the enduring strength of the Jewish spirit.

To truly grasp the impact the Holocaust had on the world is to come face-to-face with the depths of the reality of evil in the world. The events of the Holocaust will stand forever in history, for every generation to come, as a testament of the enduring responsibility for humanity — and Christians especially — to stand against the forces of evil.

It compels us to remember not only those who perished during this dark period but also every Jewish life persecuted before, during, and since this horrific chapter in history. We must ensure that such hatred, injustice, and suffering are never repeated, and commit ourselves to remain vigilant in standing against antisemitism, and all forms of evil, wherever and whenever it rears its ugly head.

CUFI's Holocaust Course is a seven-part curriculum designed to deepen your understanding of the Holocaust's historical context, conditions leading up to this reality, its lasting impact, and the significance for Christians today.

It is also an invitation to engage not only with the historical events of that time but also with testimonies of how the Jewish people rose up, against all odds and under the hand of Almighty God, and established the Third Jewish Commonwealth of Israel in 1948.

Between 1941 and 1945, through the powerful Nazi war machine, the systematic extermination of six million Jewish men, women, and children across Europe was orchestrated.

Through survivor accounts, thought-provoking reflection prompts, and a careful examination of key events, this course seeks to foster both intellectual growth and personal introspection.

Each section of the course addresses a critical aspect of post-WWI factors, beginning with the rise of Nazi antisemitism and culminating in the miraculous declaration of the establishment of the State of Israel in the very land promised by God to Abraham.

You will understand the role of state propaganda, the planning and implementation of the "Final Solution," the impact of the racial ideologies of the Nazi Third Reich, and the escalating violence against the Jewish people throughout Europe.

Moreover, you will also explore stories of survival and resistance. And how, in spite of all they endured, the Jewish people's dedication to their faith and their homeland has never changed. This stiff-necked obstinacy in the face of pure evil, after 2,000 years of exile, enabled the Jewish people to finally return to their indigenous homeland to build a Jewish state.

After surviving the realized depths of humanity's depravity, the generation whose forearms were tattooed with numbers from Auschwitz, alongside their brethren expelled from Arab lands throughout the Middle East, would ensure the promise of "Next Year in Jerusalem" can be fulfilled by every Jew, every year.

We must ensure that such hatred, injustice, and suffering are never repeated, and commit ourselves to remain vigilant in standing against antisemitism, and all forms of evil, wherever and whenever it rears its ugly head.

We must never forget the past. The trials and suffering of the Jewish people throughout history compel us to approach the present with a clear understanding of the urgent need for advocacy for Israel and the Jewish people today.

This course seeks to bridge the historical lessons of the Holocaust with the present-day responsibilities of Christians in a world where antisemitism is exponentially increasing in quantity and brutality. This course is a powerful reminder that silence and indifference allow evil to go unchallenged, while active engagement fosters hope and justice.

Studying the Holocaust and its antecedents is not merely an academic pursuit; it is a foundational step in cultivating a commitment to advocacy and meaningful action on behalf of the Jewish people.

We will remember. We will not stand silent. And we will boldly proclaim that "Never Again" is more than a phrase—it is a solemn promise we are determined to fulfill.

CUFI'S
HOLOCAUST
COURSE

THE RISE OF NAZI
ANTISEMITISM

CHRISTIANS UNITED FOR ISRAEL

THE RISE OF NAZI ANTISEMITISM

LEARNING OBJECTIVE

In this section, we will understand the origins and impacts of Nazi antisemitism, the role of propaganda, and the socioeconomic factors that fueled the rise of the Third Reich.

Nazi rally in Nuremberg, Germany, on February 1, 1936

HISTORICAL OVERVIEW
The Rise of Nazi Ideology Post-World War I

The devastation of World War I (1914–1918) profoundly reshaped Europe and the world forever. Following the war, four major empires—the Austro-Hungarian, Ottoman, German, and Russian empires—were dissolved.

New nations were established, lines in the Middle East were redrawn, and political instability and economic hardship were global. The entire world reeled from the loss of approximately 20 million lives from the Great War.

The Treaty of Versailles marked the formal conclusion of WWI, signed by the Allied Powers and Germany in 1919. It imposed reparations on Germany, including the payment of 132 billion gold marks to the Allies, stripped Germany of territories such as Alsace-Lorraine and foreign German colonies, and restricted its military to 100,000 troops.

The treaty's harsh reparations fueled national resentment, a key factor exploited by Nazi propaganda against the Jewish people.

Following WWI, Germany was in a freefall of economic collapse. Hyperinflation rendered the German mark almost worthless, wiping out the savings of millions. The Great Depression of 1929 further exacerbated the situation. Unemployment soared, and social unrest spread.

Amid this backdrop of despair, the Nazi Party offered a promise of renewal, which resonated with a disillusioned population. It also offered a scapegoat: the Jews.

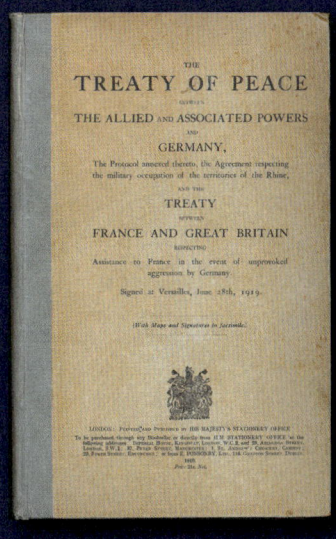

Cover of a publication of the Treaty of Versailles

———————

Adolf Hitler, the leader of the National Socialist German Workers' Party (Nazi Party), emerged. In his book *Mein Kampf* (1925), Hitler articulated a dangerous blend of ultra-nationalism, racial purity, and territorial expansion, laying the ideological foundation of the Nazi movement.

Central to Nazi ideology was antisemitism, which portrayed Jewish people as the primary source of Germany's misfortunes. Nazi propaganda, spearheaded by figures such as Joseph Goebbels, the Reich Minister of Public Enlightenment and Propaganda, disseminated hateful stereotypes through films, posters, newspapers, and speeches — swaying the hearts and minds of the entire nation.

Jews were falsely blamed for Germany's economic struggles, the spread of communism, and the decay of society. This campaign of hatred drew on longstanding antisemitic prejudices but weaponized them in new ways to rally support for the Nazi cause.

Jewish people were relentlessly demonized and accused of being the driving force behind international Marxism and what Goebbels called "immoral capitalism."[1]

A 1939 original Dutch "People's Edition" of Hitler's book *Mein Kampf*

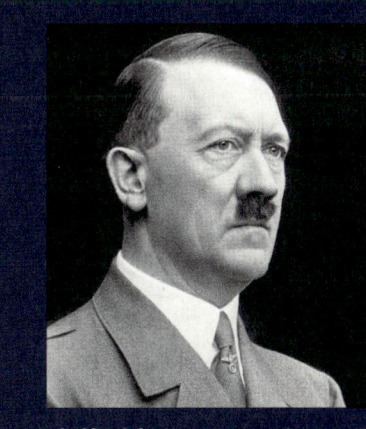

Adolf Hitler

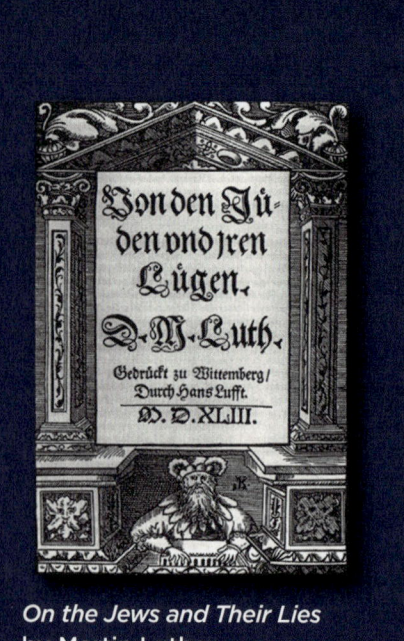

On the Jews and Their Lies by Martin Luther, published in 1543

Nazi rally at the Lustgarten in Berlin, Germany, on May 1, 1936

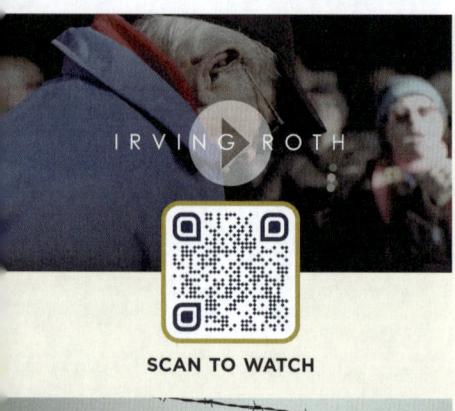

SCAN TO WATCH

SCAN TO WATCH

Hitler's antisemitism also drew from historical German sources, including the works of the composer Richard Wagner and church fathers such as John Chrysostom and Martin Luther.

Hitler crafted a narrative of scapegoating the problems of Germany upon the Jewish people. Utilizing ultranationalism rooted in historical antisemitism, he united and mobilized a fragmented society. He romanticized German nationalism while blending historic antisemitic rhetoric. Relentlessly he and the Nazi party stoked the fires of fear that the Jewish people would contaminate the "superior Aryan race." [2]

Hitler's hatred had its basis in the persecution and "othering" of Jews in European history. To him, the terrible history of murders, exclusion, and discrimination against Jews made them a natural scapegoat for the challenges in Germany post-WWI.

From the outset of taking power, the Nazi Third Reich promoted the systematic exclusion of Jews from society. This campaign that began with words culminated with action, and action led to the horrors of the Holocaust.

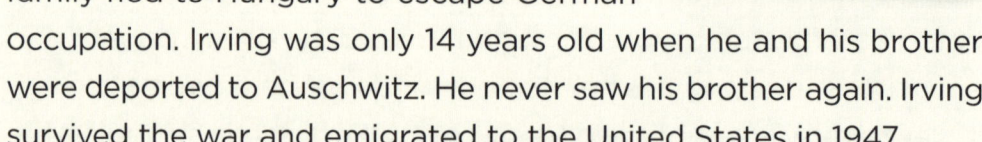

TESTIMONIAL CONNECTION

Remembering Holocaust Survivor Irving Roth

Irving Roth was born in 1929 in modern-day Slovakia. When he was eight years old, his family fled to Hungary to escape German occupation. Irving was only 14 years old when he and his brother were deported to Auschwitz. He never saw his brother again. Irving survived the war and emigrated to the United States in 1947.

For the rest of his life, he dedicated himself to educating as many people as he could about the Holocaust, the ever-present danger of antisemitism and apathy toward evil, and the power of words that can have ramifications. He was 91 years old when he passed away on February 16, 2021.

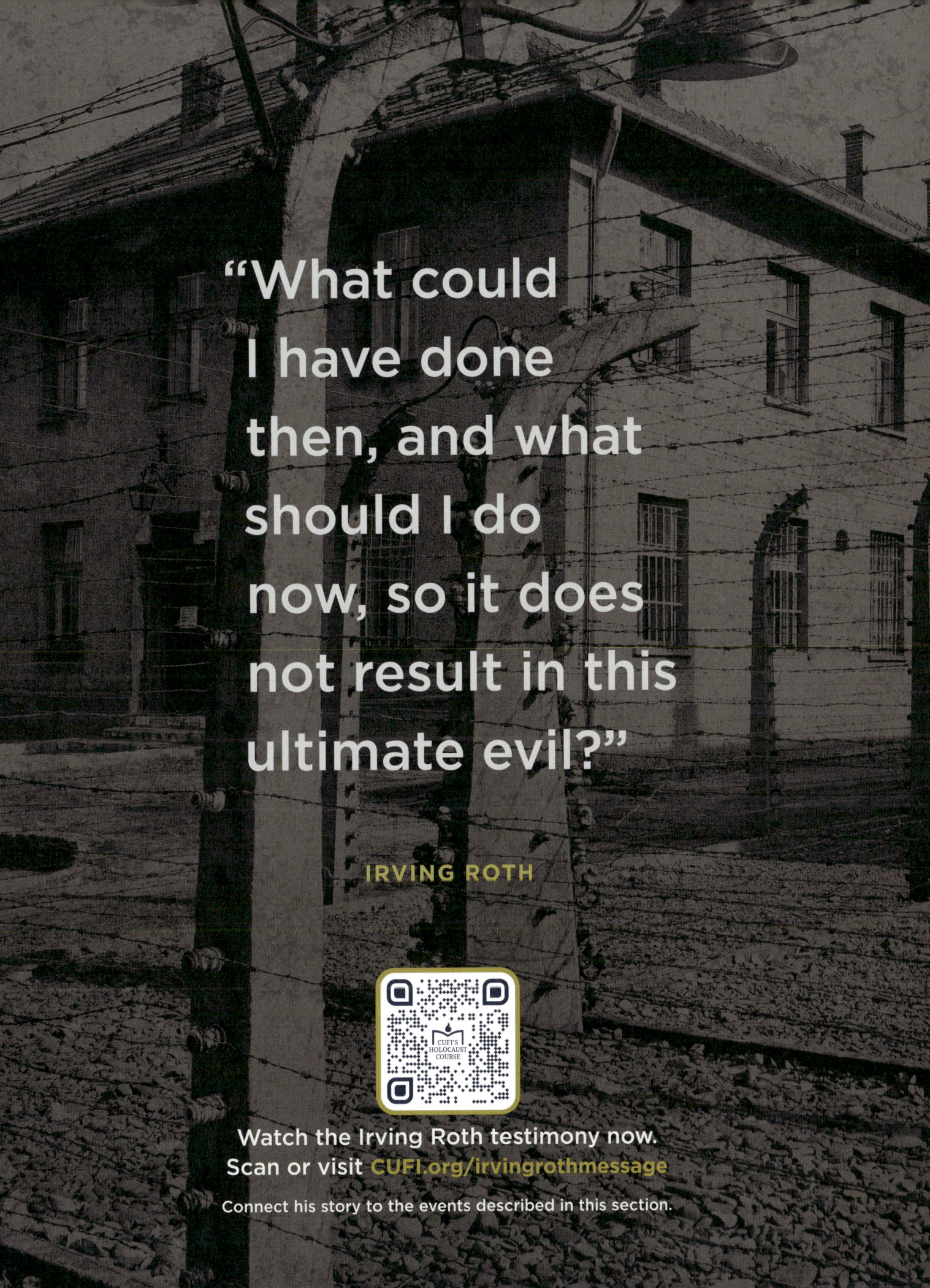

"What could I have done then, and what should I do now, so it does not result in this ultimate evil?"

IRVING ROTH

Watch the Irving Roth testimony now.
Scan or visit CUFI.org/irvingrothmessage

Connect his story to the events described in this section.

NEVER AGAIN?

SCAN TO WATCH, OR VISIT:
CUFI.org/neveragain

Adolf Hitler announces the Nuremberg Laws, 1935

KEY THEMES AND REFLECTION

By understanding and engaging with the lessons of the Holocaust, we arm ourselves with a deeper understanding of the factors that enabled such atrocities.

Loss of Rights and Humanity

The Holocaust demonstrates the devastating consequences of hatred and evil. It is also a prime example that words indeed lead to action. The Nuremberg Laws stripped the Jews of their rights, but it did not stop there. Once Jews were seen as sub-human, it eventually paved the way for what culminated in the construction of such camps as Auschwitz-Birkenau, Treblinka, and Buchenwald.

REFLECTION:

» How did early laws such as the Nuremberg Laws set the stage for later atrocities against the Jews?

The Power of Propaganda

Nazi propaganda played a pivotal role in dehumanizing Jewish people and justifying persecution and violence. From weekly tabloids such as *Der Stürmer* (*the Attacker*), which spread degrading caricatures, false accusations, and conspiracy theories against the Jews, to films including *The Eternal Jew*, that portrayed Jews as corrupt and dangerous, the Nazis wielded propaganda ruthlessly.

REFLECTION:

» How can the media we consume shape our perception of other people groups?

Resilience Amidst Adversity

Holocaust museums the world over tell the story of the atrocities and pain the Jewish people suffered. But another undeniable truth to the history of the Holocaust is the incredible stories of courage and resilience of the Jewish people. Their stories of survival, resistance, and rebuilding after the war highlight the strength of the Jewish spirit and the power of hope.

REFLECTION:

>> How can the resilience of Holocaust survivors inspire us to face challenges in our own lives?

INTERACTION EXERCISE

Understanding the rise of Nazi antisemitism is essential to grasping how hatred and unchecked propaganda can spiral into widespread persecution and hate. Understanding the power of Nazi antisemitic propaganda will deepen your knowledge and equip you to identify similar patterns of hatred you may encounter today.

STUDY:

>> Propaganda posters depicted Jews as grotesque or subhuman. An oft seen slogan was "The Jew is the enemy."

>> A children's book published in 1938 titled *Der Giftpilz* (*The Poisonous Mushroom*) used cartoons and stories to spread antisemitic ideas.

>> Leni Riefenstahl's film *Triumph of the Will* (1935) glorified the Nazi regime and ideology. It bolstered the Nazi Ideal while integrating antisemitic tones.

>> Nazi-controlled newspapers such as *Völkischer Beobachter* (*People's Observer*) printed antisemitic articles and conspiracy theories against the Jews.

A sign displaying the words *"Arbeit Macht Frei"* ("Work makes one free") at the main entrance to Auschwitz, the largest of the concentration camps

Example of an *antisemitisches wahlplakat* (antisemitic election poster)

A children's book published in 1938 titled *Der Giftpilz* (*The Poisonous Mushroom*)

15

Der Stürmer, 1944:
a significant part of
Nazi propaganda and
vehemently antisemitic

>> The Nazis used massive rallies as powerful propaganda tools. Events were meticulously organized to inspire loyalty and awe in the regime. Symbols of power, such as the swastika and SS uniforms, were utilized, as well as the power of music with anthems and bands. Synchronized marches, salutes, climactic oratorial speeches, glorification of Hitler as the Führer, and night rallies that included torches, spotlights, and bonfires to heighten the emotional effect.

Nazi rally at Heldenplatz Square in Vienna, Austria, on March 14, 1941

Nazi Sturmabteilung (SA)
military enforcers for the
Nazi Party, marching in a
rally known as the Nazi Party
Congress in Nuremberg
(Nazi Germany, 1934)

INITIATE:

Look up the local synagogue in your city or area. On the "Contact Us" page, write a short note introducing yourself as a Christian who supports Israel. Consider reaching out to drop off a gift and a card of support. You may be surprised at how much even such a small gesture toward friendship will be received with gratitude.

CREATE:

Imagine the year is 1939. You are a German Jew living in the middle of Nazi Germany. Though born in Germany, since you are Jewish, you are no longer a citizen. You can no longer vote, display the German flag at your home, or even walk around a

Jewish Star

public park. Your Jewish family members and friends who were lawyers, doctors, teachers, or civil servants have all lost their jobs. Your Jewish friends have been expelled from the public universities. Write a short reflection of what it feels like to see your country change before your eyes.

ENGAGE FURTHER

Watch the video in the sidebar. As you watch, imagine what it would have been like to be Jewish in Europe in the years between WWI and WWII.

As antisemitism gained ground, how do you think you would have reacted? What signs do you see today that mirror that period?

REFLECTION AND ACTION

What began as antisemitic rhetoric in the 1930s quickly escalated from speeches on platforms to the dehumanization of a people to the murder of millions. What about today? The transport of civilians on train cars to death camps, the extermination of Jewish ghettos and communities, and the horrific loss of life during WWII all took place less than 100 years ago.

Antisemitism does not stop with words. It twists hearts and, in the end, leads to violence against the Jewish people. Hatred, indifference, and fear can lead to unimaginable consequences in our day as well.

The Holocaust is not just a story of tragedy that happened once long ago. The stories are still alive today, and the lessons are still relevant. The warnings we can learn from those who lived before us can still shape our future today.

Holocaust survivors are some of the most incredible people who have ever lived. They lived through unimaginable pain and suffering, survived, and looked forward. They fought to rebuild their lives and create a brighter future for their families and generations that would follow.

THE RISE OF NAZI ANTISEMITISM

In this video, learn how Hitler managed to turn most Germans against the Jewish people, demonizing them with rhetoric that turned friends against friends and neighbors against neighbors.

SCAN TO WATCH, OR VISIT:
CUFI.org/holocaustcourse

Railway cars used to transport Jewish men and women to Nazi camps

We must never forget their stories, voices, and names. Their testimony of life compels us to stand as witnesses for the future.

The Holocaust reminds us that silence and apathy have devastating consequences. But with a knowledge of history and an understanding that apathy can lead to devastation, you can equip yourself to stand as an advocate for the Jewish people, for life, and against the advancement of evil in the world.

Consider how the lessons of the Holocaust apply today. By engaging with the reality of the past, we honor the memory of those who lost their lives and recommit ourselves once more to combatting antisemitism in all its forms today.

"Hall of Names" at Yad Vashem, the World Holocaust Remembrance Center in Jerusalem, Israel

Pastor Hagee speaking at the first CUFI meeting (February 2006) to establish the mission to support and defend Israel

REFLECT:
» How can the power of media be utilized to influence people toward good or evil?
» How does the documentary *Never Again?* apply to the modern world?
» What can you practically do today to combat antisemitism in your community?

JOURNAL:
Write a journal entry to your future self. What do you want to have accomplished in 10 years that actively combatted antisemitism in your life? What do you want your legacy to be?

CONSIDER:
» What are some ways we, as Christians, can stand with Israel and the Jewish people?
» What are some ways we can get involved with the programs Christians United for Israel already has in place?

Glossary of Terms:

ANTISEMITISM:
A certain perception of Jews, which may be expressed as hatred toward Jews. Rhetorical and physical manifestations of antisemitism are directed toward Jewish or non-Jewish individuals and/or their property, toward Jewish community institutions and religious facilities.

NUREMBERG LAWS:
A set of laws enacted by Nazi Germany in 1935 that drastically restricted the rights of Jews. The laws stripped Jews of citizenship, segregated them from society, and paved the way for further persecution.

THIRD REICH:
The term used to describe the Nazi regime in Germany from January 30, 1933, to May 8, 1945.

TREATY OF VERSAILLES:
The treaty signed at the Palace of Versailles in June of 1919 between the Allies and Germany, marking the end of WWI.

NOTES

NOTES

"Moral responsibility
calls out to
every generation:

If not you, **who?**

If not now, **when?**

If not your
generation, **whose?**"

INSPIRED BY HILLEL THE ELDER

NAZI RACIAL IDEOLOGIES

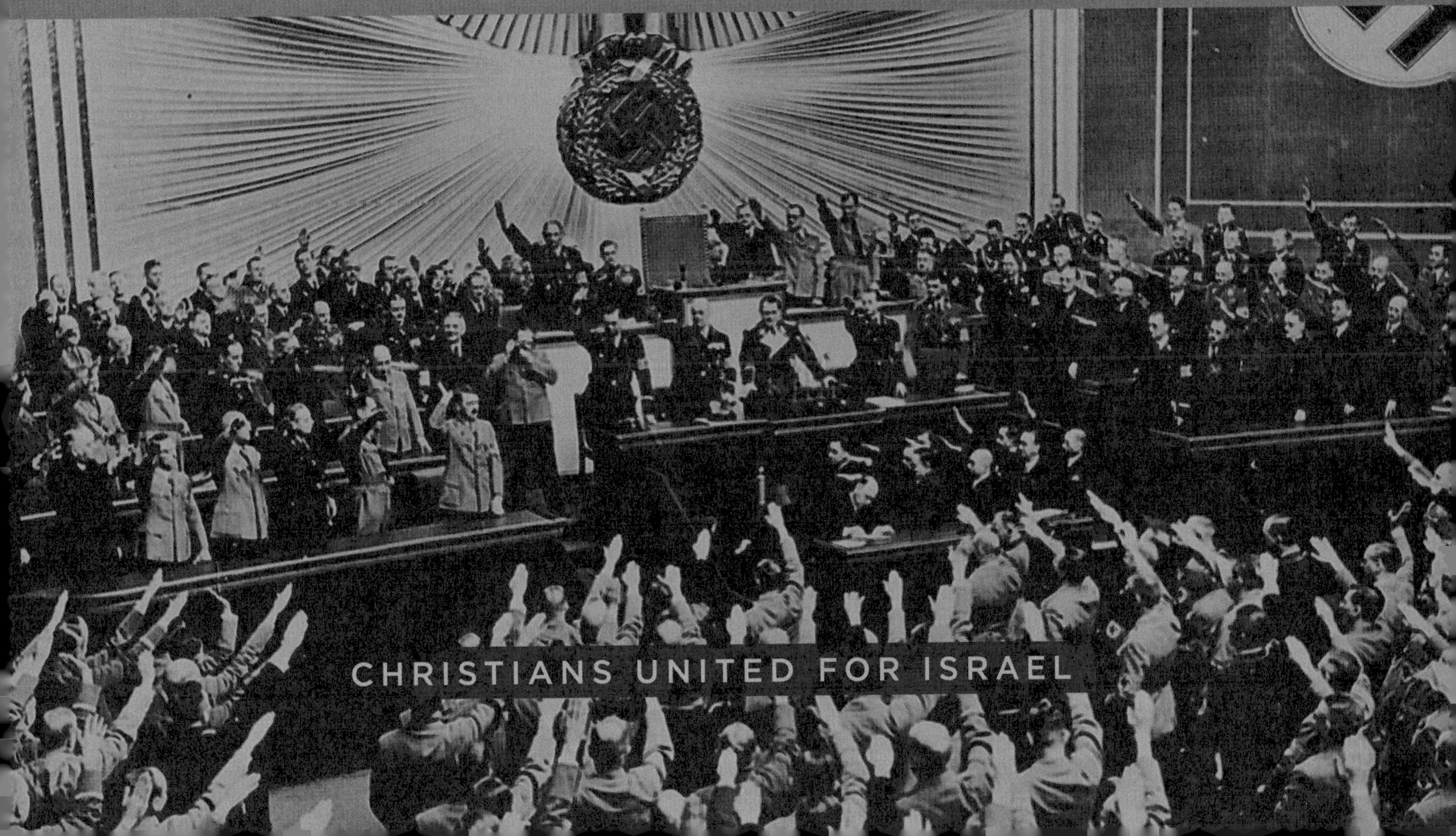

NAZI RACIAL IDEOLOGIES

LEARNING OBJECTIVE

In this section, we will explore the origins and effects of Nazi racial ideologies, tracing their historical roots and devastating consequences, which culminated in the Holocaust.

German Chancellor Adolf Hitler being welcomed by supporters at Nuremberg, circa 1933

HISTORICAL OVERVIEW

When Adolf Hitler and the Nazi Party came to power in 1933, Germany was experiencing economic breakdown, political instability, and widespread disillusionment. The Nazis immediately began a nationwide campaign of toxic ideology that promoted the supremacy of the Aryan race and squarely placed blame for Germany's problems on the Jews.

Nazi ideology centered on the belief in and adherence to a strict racial hierarchy. Germans of Aryan descent were placed at the top of the order, while Jews were portrayed as subhuman as a race, corrupt, dangerous, vile, and the primary enemy of the German people.

These racial ideologies were not new. The Nazis drew on pseudo scientific theories which claimed to classify human races based on physical and intellectual traits. For example, the French work *Essai sur l'inégalité des Races Humaines* (*Essay on the Inequality of the Human Races*) by Arthur de Gobineau, which argued the superiority of the white race, was published in the 1850s. *The Foundations of the Nineteenth Century* by Chamberlain discussed Aryan superiority and the dangers of the Jews, as did portions of Nietzsche's *The Will to Power* and Darwin's *Social Darwinism*.

In addition to the economic scapegoating which blamed Jews for the financial crises in Germany, the Nazis also built on long-standing antisemitic stereotypes, including medieval accusations such as blood libel — the false claim that Jews used the blood of Christian children to make Matzah bread.

The combination of antisemitic rhetoric with intense propaganda was catastrophic for the Jewish community. The Nazis constructed a worldview that painted the Jews as less than human, dangerous to society, and marked for annihilation. They justified discrimination, open persecution, and ultimately, mass genocide.

The Eternal Jew *(Der ewige Jude)*, an antisemitic Nazi propaganda film commissioned by Joseph Goebbels in 1940

Child vendor in Jewish ghetto

ELEMENTS OF NAZI RACIAL IDEOLOGY

1. ARYAN SUPREMACY

The Nazis glorified the Aryan race as the pinnacle of human perfection — pure, noble, and biologically superior. Drawing from distorted 19th- and 20th-century racial theories, they idealized Aryans as tall, athletic, blond-haired, blue-eyed, and fair-skinned. Nazi propaganda reinforced this image, portraying Aryans as uniquely creative, intelligent, and destined to rule. This false narrative served as a justification for their policies of racial purity and expansion, portraying the Aryan race as the natural rulers of a global hierarchy.

2. ANTISEMITISM

Antisemitism was the cornerstone of Nazi ideology, forming the basis of their policies and propaganda. Jews bore the blame

Die PARTEI (The Party)

A sculpture that was installed at the Reich Chancellery in Berlin, symbolizing the spirit of the Nazi Party

Children at Auschwitz

for Germany's problems and even the nation's defeat in World War I. The Nazis blamed Jews for the spread of communism (referred to as "Judeo-Bolshevism") and portrayed them as greedy, corrupt, and responsible for societal decay. What began with dehumanization laid the groundwork for what would later lead to the systematic liquidation of Jewish communities. Nazi propaganda intensified prejudice against the Jews, depicting them as evil and the underlying corrupting force undermining the ideal national values of Germany.

3. EUGENICS AND RACIAL PURITY

Central to Nazi policy was the embracing of eugenics — a pseudo scientific movement aimed at improving the genetic quality of the human population. Inspired by earlier eugenics theories, the Nazis sought to create a racially pure society by promoting the reproduction of racially valuable Aryan families while systematically eliminating those deemed inferior. Individuals considered unfit underwent forced sterilization. These measures, as well as the extermination of marginalized groups, were central to the Nazi regime's vision of racial purity and what was portrayed as the biological improvement of the German population.

4. RACIAL HIERARCHIES

A key to understanding Nazi racial hierarchy is what the Nazis termed *Übermensch* and *Untermensch.* The *Übermensch* (superman) was portrayed as the physically, intellectually, and morally superior man, destined to rule others. This was the pinnacle found in Aryan supremacy as the master race. On the contrary, the *Untermensch* (subhuman) were those who were racially, biologically, and in every way inferior. As subhuman and unfit for life, they must make way for the *Übermensch.* With that worldview, the logical steps were vilification, marginalization, and in the end, eradication and genocide on a massive scale.

5. *LEBENSRAUM* (LIVING SPACE)

The ideology of *Lebensraum* centered on the desire for German territorial expansion to secure land and resources for the master

Aryan race (*Herrenvolk*). The Nazis believed that Germany's growth required the conquest of vast swaths of land, with justification to exterminate entire populations in their wake, to make room for German settlers to establish the Greater German Reich. It was a geopolitical strategy of expansion and a racial agenda used to justify the enslavement, displacement, and mass murder of millions under the Nazi regime.

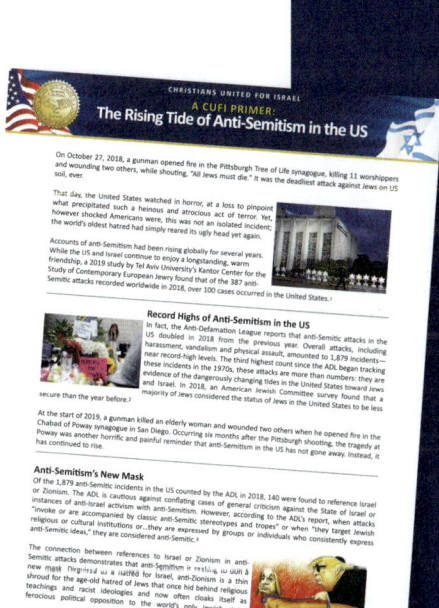

Deportation to Treblinka

Each of these contributed to the systemic persecution and eventual mass violence that characterized the Nazi regime, culminating in the Holocaust. Due to Nazi ideology, a reign of institutionalized terror against the Jewish people began as they were forced into ghettos, deprived of basic rights, subjected to forced labor, and killed.

TESTIMONIAL CONNECTION

In the 1920s, the Weimar Republic was in power in Germany. The country was in unrest after WWI, and antisemitism was widespread and growing. Jews were blamed for the turmoil in the country and anti-Jewish propaganda was flourishing in media, politics, and society. The Nazi party was beginning to get more and more traction.

Now 100 years later, antisemitism is still alive across America and the world. And it is growing. After October 2023, antisemitism skyrocketed, rising by more than 300% across the U.S. The number of antisemitic incidents reached levels unseen since the days leading up to WWII.

Read the CUFI primer, *The Rising Tide of Antisemitism in the US*. What does antisemitism look like in America today? What can you do in your circle of influence to fight against it?

SCAN TO DOWNLOAD

KEY THEMES AND REFLECTION

The endgame of Nazi racial ideology found its zenith in what became known as the Final Solution. The Final Solution was the systematic plan for the full extermination of the Jewish population throughout Europe. The plan was implemented in stages, beginning with mass shootings by mobile killing units (*Einsatzgruppen*) in Eastern Europe and escalating to the construction of extermination camps such as Auschwitz, Treblinka, and Sobibor.

The Final Solution involved the use of industrial methods to carry out mass genocide and became a key centerpiece of the Nazi war machine. It included gas chambers, forced labor, starvation, and medical experiments. By 1945, six million Jews had been murdered under the plan, as they were viewed as racially undesirable and enemies of the state.

Nazi racial ideologies began with creating new worldviews, which led to abusive policies, which, in turn, inevitably gave way to violence. After the Nuremberg Laws were passed, it was only a matter of time before the Final Solution would be approved. It is a sobering reminder of the destructive power of hate and the profound importance of standing against evil.

The Danger of Dehumanization

Nazi racial ideologies thrived on the dehumanization of entire people groups. By reducing people to be seen as subhuman, less than, and dangerous, oppressors seek to justify atrocities.

"Free Palestine" has become a slogan of antisemitism and hatred against Israel and the Jewish people

> **REFLECTION:**
> ›› What parallels do you see between the dehumanization tactics used by the Nazis in the 1930s and the marches and protests of modern-day antisemitism in cities and on college campuses?

The Role of Propaganda

Nazi propaganda was instrumental in spreading racial ideologies, shaping public opinion, silencing dissent, and presenting a constant stream of Nazi messaging — leading the entire nation into the throes of evil.

REFLECTION:

» When you open your social media accounts, listen to podcasts, or read news headlines, what themes do you see regarding the Jewish people? Is the predominant theme that of acceptance or vilification toward the Jews?

"Farfur" was a character created by Hamas for the children's show *Tomorrow's Pioneers* that promoted violence against Jews and *jihad* against Israel

Moral Responsibility

The Holocaust stands forever on the stage of history as a memorial etched in stone, calling out to the generations to come to remember. Remember what mankind was capable of perpetrating. And take one step further: act. When evil raises its head, whether in rhetoric or action, have the courage to take up the moral responsibility to stand against it. If not you, who? If not now, when? If not your generation, whose?

REFLECTION:

» In what ways can you, either as an individual or connected and empowered within the context of a like-minded community of Christians, act courageously to stand in defense of the Jewish people throughout the world?

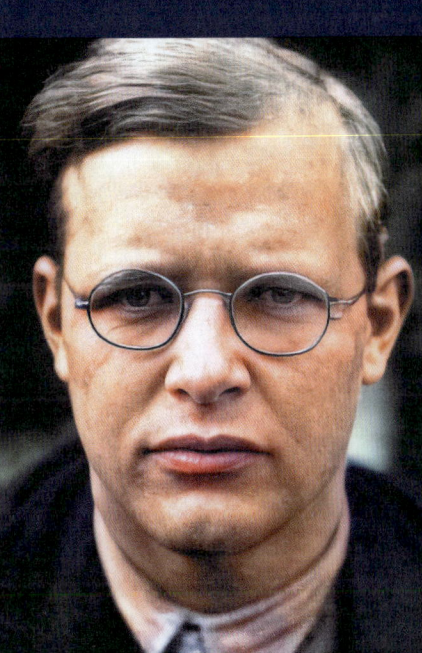

Dietrich Bonhoeffer:

German theologian, pastor, and anti-Nazi dissident who opposed the Nazi regime. A member of the German resistance movement, he participated in a plot to assassinate Hitler. He was imprisoned and executed by the Nazis in April 1945.

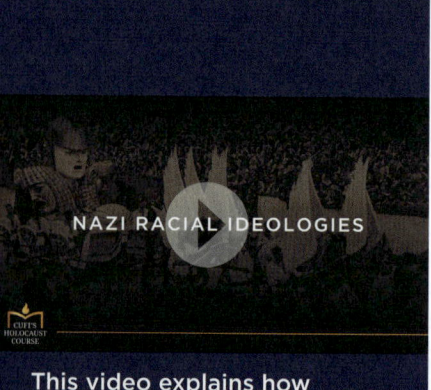

NAZI RACIAL IDEOLOGIES

This video explains how Hitler used propaganda and seduction to convince millions of Germans that the Jews were responsible for all the nation's problems after World War I.

SCAN TO WATCH, OR VISIT:
CUFI.org/holocaustcourse

INTERACTION EXERCISE

If you want to know the future, investigate the past. The stories from the annals of history tend to repeat themselves in upcoming generations. Too often we forget the lessons of those who lived before us, but if we study the pages of history, we can learn to find our place of impact today.

DISCUSS:

» What lessons can we learn from the generation that lived in Europe from 1920 to 1940?

» How do stories from history challenge us to think about our role as Christians who support Israel today?

RESEARCH:

» Look through various news outlets, either online or in print. Search for terms such as "Israel," "Jewish," or "Zionist." What kinds of articles come up? What kinds of trends do you see? What stands out to you?

CONSIDER:

» Come up with one way you could show support for Israel or the Jewish people, either online or in person, in your sphere of influence. What ideas come to mind?

ENGAGE FURTHER

To go deeper, spend some time **watching the video**. These stories reveal the devastating impact of Nazi propaganda and inspire us to stand against antisemitism and injustice in our world today.

REFLECTION AND ACTION

The construction of gas chambers and concentration camps did not begin in a vacuum. The murder of millions of Jews did not happen overnight. The Holocaust was the predictable and intentional progression of action that was taken after decades of propaganda, hate, and dehumanization of the Jewish people.

Racial ideology was used as a powerful tool. First the Jewish people were marginalized. They were portrayed as dangerous, as corrupt, as vile, as evil, and as the reason for the problems in the entire nation of Germany.

First, Nazi ideology taught their people to be disgusted by the Jews, then to hate them, then to justify their eradication. Words are powerful. Belief is powerful. Ideology and worldview are powerful. They always lead to action, whether for good or for evil.

Consider the state of the world today in regard to antisemitism. Consider how Jews are portrayed in the media. What do you see today that perhaps the German people were seeing 100 years ago?

What happens when good people say nothing in the face of evil?

There are so many opportunities to take action through Christians United for Israel. How can you help combat antisemitism in your generation?

Israeli flag at the Western Wall in Jerusalem, Israel

Supporting Israel isn't just about agreement; it's about action. **Take a step** today to make a difference in your community, state, and nation.

SCAN TO WATCH, OR VISIT:
CUFI.org/engage/act

Glossary of Terms:

EINSATZGRUPPEN:
Mobile killing units formed by Nazi Germany, primarily composed of SS and police personnel. These units operated in occupied territories during World War II, carrying out mass shootings of Jews, Roma, political prisoners, and others considered undesirable by the Nazi regime. Einsatzgruppen were instrumental in the early stages of the Holocaust, often following the German army into newly conquered areas to systematically exterminate local populations.

HERRENVOLK (MASTER RACE):
A Nazi term describing the Aryan race as the master race. Within the Nazi racial ideology, they believed and propagated the idea that the higher Herrenvolk were destined to rule.

LEBENSRAUM (LIVING SPACE):
A Nazi policy advocating greater territorial expansion. As the Nazis believed they were the master race, the policy of lebensraum justified conquering other peoples and land and confiscating resources to provide for the German master race.

ÜBERMENSCH (SUPERMAN):
A concept promoted by the Nazis to promote the ideology of Aryan racial superiority over all other races. The "Übermensch" was the idealized, superior Aryan figure destined to dominate and rule over lesser races.

UNTERMENSCH (SUBHUMAN):
A term used by the Nazis to dehumanize groups they considered inferior, such as Jews, as part of their racist worldview. Once they convinced people that there were subhuman, less-than people, it was easier to justify persecuting, hating, and ultimately, killing them.

NOTES

NOTES

KRISTALLNACHT AND EARLY PERSECUTION IN EUROPE

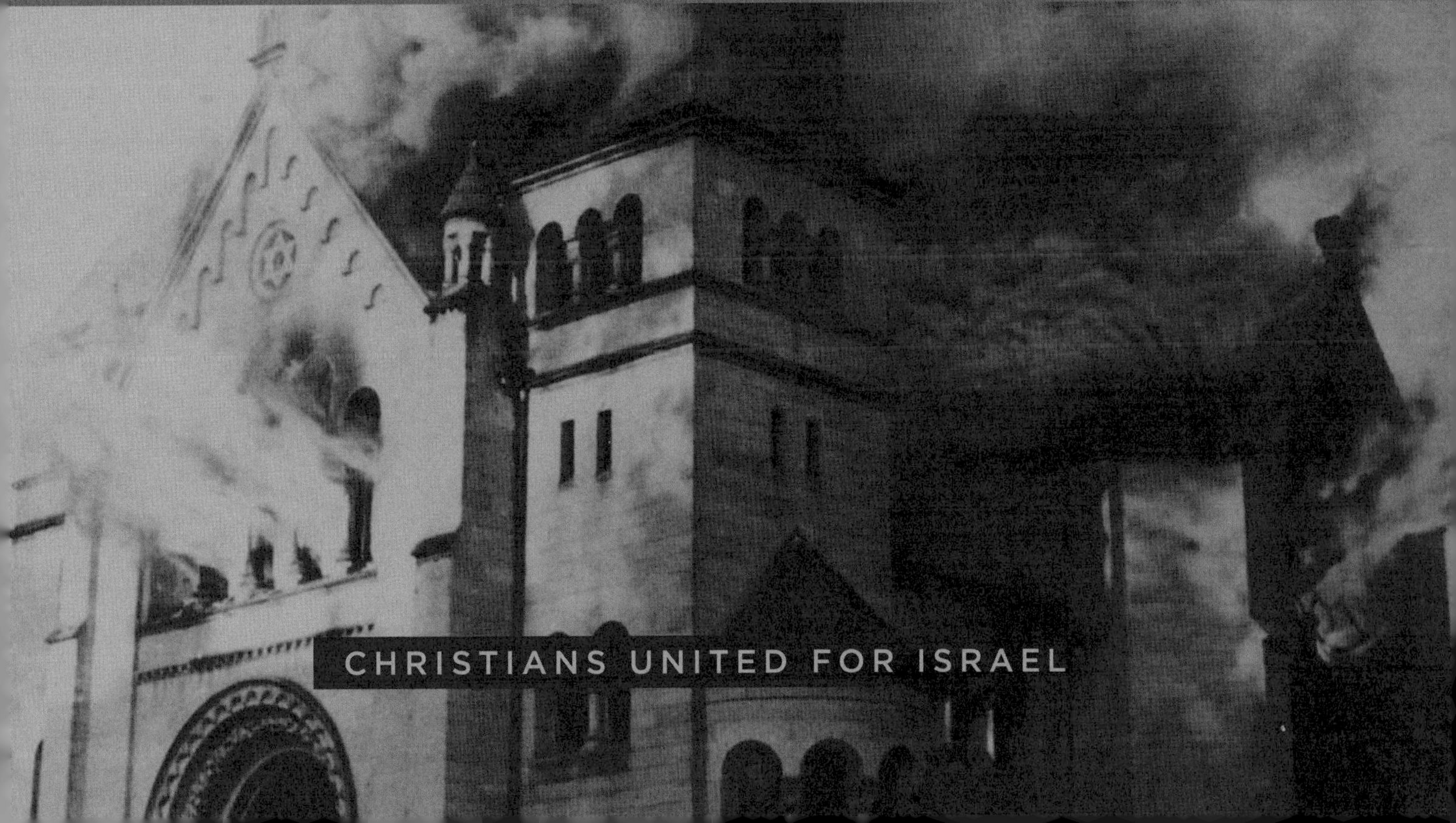

KRISTALLNACHT AND EARLY PERSECUTION IN EUROPE

LEARNING OBJECTIVE

In this section, we will explore how Kristallnacht (the "Night of Broken Glass") was the tipping point that set the stage for persecution of the Jewish people and what would eventually culminate with the Holocaust.

SS soldier posts a sign on a Jewish-owned shop on Friedrichstrasse, a central shopping area in Berlin, warning Germans not to buy Jewish goods

HISTORICAL OVERVIEW

Kristallnacht, or the "Night of Broken Glass," on November 9–10, 1938, marked a watershed moment in Nazi Germany. It shattered the illusion of safety for Jewish citizens and signaled the beginning of state-sanctioned, systematic persecution, carried out with impunity.

The Nazis were looking for a reason to incite the German population at large toward violence against the Jewish population. They wanted a pogrom but needed a pretense to begin one.

The Nazis found what they were looking for in Paris. Thousands of Polish Jews had been expelled to the Polish-German border and left in dire conditions. In protest, Herschel Grynszpan, a 17-year-old Polish Jew, shot Ernst vom Rath, a German diplomat in Paris. In response, the Nazis unleashed hell upon the entire Jewish population across Nazi-controlled cities.

Over the course of two days, no Jew was safe. It was a state-sponsored open season against the Jewish population, backed by government resources. In German the operation was called *Novemberpogrome* with active participation from the Nazi Party Sturmabteilung (SA) and Schutzstaffel (SS) paramilitary forces, Hitler Youth, and German civilians.

Jewish homes were looted and ransacked, over 7,000 Jewish businesses were destroyed, 92 Jews were killed, 267 synagogues were ruined or burned, and approximately 30,000 Jewish men were arrested and deported to concentration camps at Sachsenhausen, Dachau, and Buchenwald.

———

Kristallnacht, in many respects, was the beginning of the Holocaust. It was the key event that transitioned the German population from economic or social oppression and marginalization of the Jews to violence, brutality, and murder.

Kristallnacht occurred five years after Hitler's rise to power and three years after the Nuremberg Laws institutionalized antisemitic policies. For years, the Nazi regime had cultivated a culture of hatred through relentless propaganda and systematic scapegoating of the Jewish people.

Now, the Jewish population had been subjugated by institutionalized racial discrimination and the loss of rights, citizenship, and freedom. Germany was under Nazi power, and Jews were without protection from crimes or violence against them. The Nazi-led government was actively stoking the fire of hatred against the Jews.

A synagogue in Hanover on fire in November of 1938

Map of synagogues destroyed on Kristallnacht [3]

German citizens walk past a Jewish business destroyed during Kristallnacht [4]

Jews rounded up in Stadthagen after Kristallnacht

Gasoline being poured over the pews of a synagogue

Nazi members carrying Jewish books away for burning or destruction on November 9, 1938

Kristallnacht not only intensified persecution but normalized public violence against Jewish citizens, emboldened by government approval and oversight.

By the morning of November 11, 1938, a new normal had dawned throughout Nazi Germany. The Jewish population was devastated and no longer had any remnant of hope left that they would one day regain the life or the freedom or the rights they once enjoyed. They understood there was no future left for a Jew in Nazi Germany.

TESTIMONIAL CONNECTION

Front page of the *Sunday Express* November 13, 1938

Kristallnacht was a death blow to the Jewish population in every sense of the word. As the *Sunday Express* reported: German Jews were ordered to pay one billion Reichsmarks for the damage of the riots, banned from owning businesses, and barred from society.

Any insurance claim filed would be confiscated by the state; anyone who had property damaged must immediately repair it at their own cost. Beginning January 1 of 1939, Jews were forbidden to own or manage a shop, factory, or any other kind of business.

Imagine your family owned a watch shop. The shop had been in your family for three generations, situated in the city center of Berlin, and you were set to inherit it and run it one day. On Kristallnacht, it was destroyed; the synagogue you attended since birth was burned to the ground, and half the people in your life were arrested and deported, and you don't know where they went. Write a journal entry to yourself that you don't think anyone will ever read. What would you write?

KEY THEMES AND REFLECTION

The events of Kristallnacht and the overt persecution of Jews in Europe revealed the devastating consequences of unchecked hatred. The stories and pictures are a torch of remembrance, shining through the hallways of time, calling out to us today to remember what happens when good men and women are silent and when evil is left to have its way.

Kristallnacht is an example that shows with vivid clarity how quickly mankind can fall to acts of atrocity when they are not stopped. There was no one left standing to defend the Jewish people. They had no protection, they had no rule of law to guard them, and furthermore, their own government was sponsoring terror and horror upon them.

The Point of No Return

Kristallnacht was a devastating event that made clear the Nazis' (and the greater population of Germany's) willingness and capacity to escalate persecution of the Jewish people from social, legal, and economic pressure to all-out violence and brutality to the point of murder.

The Role of Indifference

While newspapers worldwide reported on the plight of Jewish communities, global apathy and indifference prevailed. Despite widespread knowledge of the violence, imprisonment, and murder, the international community remained largely silent.

The Call to Faith and Action

As Christians, we are reminded of the exhortation to resist and withstand evil in the world today, as well as the Biblical mandate to support Israel and the Jewish people, even if the entire world turns against them.

The New York Times, November 11, 1938

People watching as arrested Jews are led through the streets of Baden-Baden, guarded by police and SS men on November 10, 1938, after Kristallnacht (The Night of Broken Glass)

Civilians watching a Nazi officer on Kristallnacht vandalize a Jewish property

A Jewish woman after Kristallnacht in Stadthagen

REFLECTION:

» How was Kristallnacht a reflection of years of antisemitic propaganda and policies in Nazi Germany?

» Consider the role of bystanders during Kristallnacht. They looked on but did nothing, either for fear of retribution or because they silently condoned the actions of the raving mobs. Were bystanders equally complicit?

» Why is it important for Christians to speak out against antisemitism today?

INTERACTION EXERCISE

SURVIVOR VOICES

On the morning of November 9, 1938, Carol (Mannheimer) Selig-Kinderman was 14 years old. The police arrested her father and brother and broke into her house. She said:

"They slashed all the sofas and beds, broke down all the closets, the mirrors. They cut off the legs of our dining table. Because they smashed our windows, we were also very cold. Later, through the smashed windows, I heard the SS marching under our house and debating whether they should burn down our house. Eventually, they realized we lived next door to a high-ranking Nazi, so they decided not to do it. My parents owned a winery and had special sets of wine glasses in all sizes, 144 glasses in all. They smashed them all." [5]

Klaus Langer wrote a diary entry on November 11, 1938:

"At three o'clock the synagogue and the Jewish youth center were put on fire. Then they began to destroy Jewish businesses. During the morning, private homes also were being demolished. Fires were started at single homes belonging to Jews. At six-thirty in the morning the Gestapo came to our home and arrested Father and Mother...In the middle of the night, at 2:30 A.M., the Storm Troopers [Sturmabteilung, or SA, also known as the Brownshirts] smashed windows and threw stones against store shutters. After a few minutes they demanded to be let into the house."[6]

David Buffum, U.S. consul to the city of Leipzig, wrote a report after the events:

"At 3 A.M. November 10, 1938, was unleashed a barrage of Nazi ferocity as had had no equal hitherto in Germany, or very likely anywhere else in the world...Jewish dwellings were smashed into and contents demolished or looted."[7]

WRITE OR DISCUSS WITH OTHERS:
» How do stories like these help us understand the impact of Kristallnacht?
» Why is it critical that Christians take a stand against antisemitism?

CREATIVE RESPONSE

Imagine you are a Jewish young adult living in Germany in 1938. Create a work of art or write a poem or lyrics to a song of lament of what just happened to your city, your community, and your life. Describe what you saw, what you heard, and your feelings as you look out over the aftermath. What kinds of emotions come up? What are your fears for the future? What hope is left?

Share your reflections in a journal entry or with a discussion group.

"Synagogues were burned down on Kristallnacht, and the world stood by and remained silent." — Shmuel Rosenman, chairman of the International March of the Living

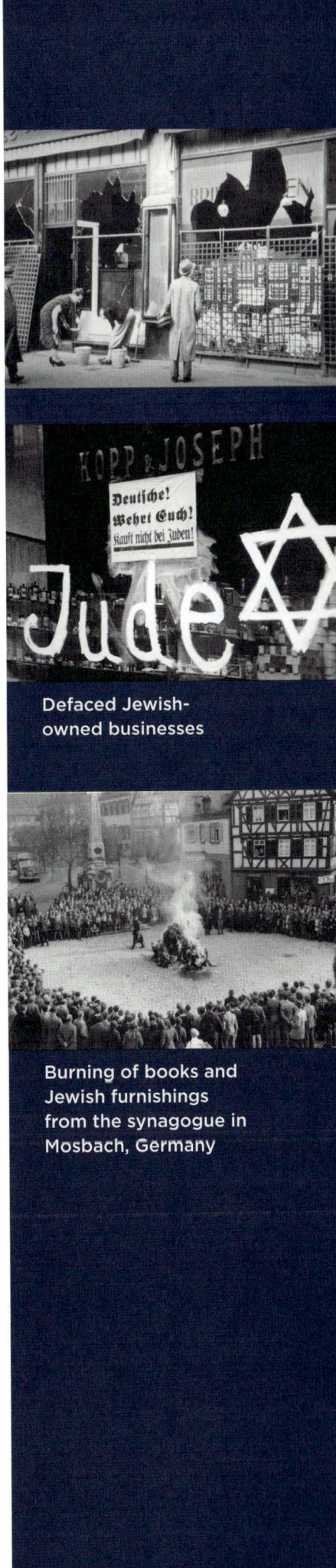

Defaced Jewish-owned businesses

Burning of books and Jewish furnishings from the synagogue in Mosbach, Germany

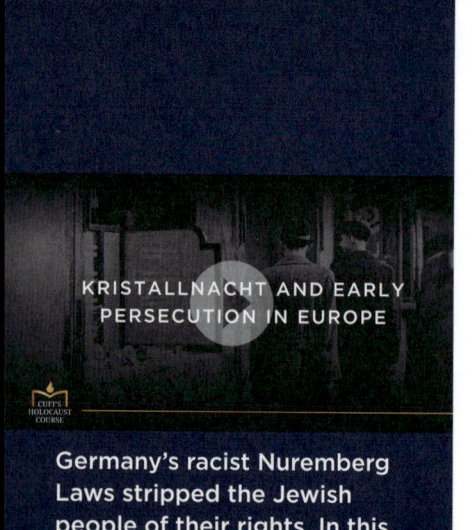

KRISTALLNACHT AND EARLY PERSECUTION IN EUROPE

Germany's racist Nuremberg Laws stripped the Jewish people of their rights. In this video, learn how these laws encouraged and pressured ordinary Germans to partici- pate in persecuting Jews.

SCAN TO WATCH, OR VISIT:
CUFI.org/holocaustcourse

Vandalism on the northwest gate of the White House on November 4, 2023, after thousands of anti- Israel protesters marched in Washington, D.C.

ENGAGE FURTHER

Watch the video. How do these stories of what happened that fateful night challenge you to consider how you can combat antisemitism today?

REFLECTION AND ACTION

The events of Kristallnacht did not happen in a vacuum. The Nazi government in power and the populace in general did not wake up one morning and simultaneously decide to begin a pogrom against tens of thousands of Jews across multiple cities, towns, and even multiple countries.

By November 1938, antisemitism had already taken root and flourished through marginalization, vilification, and persecution of Jewish communities. Books, films, posters, speeches, and legal action restricting the freedom of Jews had already been rolled out.

A culture of hatred, fear, and perceived disgust with the Jewish population had been injected into the psyche of the German people for years. Little by little, step by step, a wall of hatred and lies had been constructed.

Violent action was a foregone conclusion. It was only a matter of time before the Nazi government moved from rhetoric to brutality, from propaganda to pogrom.

In our day, we are seeing both antisemitic propaganda against the Jewish people worldwide and violent action. Antisemitic incidents are commonplace in Europe and America.

Following the brutal October 7th Hamas Massacre, during which the terrorist group murdered, tortured, and kid- napped their way through southern Israel, antisemitic incidents surged worldwide, including across the United States. On many college campuses, protests erupted that openly supported the violence against Israel, creat- ing a hostile environment for Jewish students. Antisemitic

Anti-Israel protesters rallied at Columbia University, forming a "Gaza Solidarity Encampment." Similar protests and sit-ins emerged nationwide in the wake of Hamas' horrific October 7 attack against Israel. Reports of violent acts targeting Jewish students follow many such protests.

slogans, harassment, and displays of hate were rampant, as many universities failed to protect Jewish students or condemn the horrific acts of terror.

It is not a time for silence or apathy. Many all around the world are taught to hate Israel and the Jewish people. They chant, "From the river to the sea, Palestine will be free." What they are calling for is a genocide of the entire Jewish people. It is time to stand and be counted. It is the day to rise in defense of Israel.

When King Ahasuerus had issued a decree on the suggestion of Haman that every Jew throughout his kingdom be destroyed, Mordechai came to Esther and asked her to help. He said:

> *"For if you remain completely silent at this time, relief and deliverance will arise for the Jews from another place, but you and your father's house will perish. Yet who knows whether you have come to the kingdom for such a time as this?"* (Esther 4:14, NKJV).

Esther answered the call of her day, and the Jewish people were delivered. May we be those who answer the call in ours as well. May we be those who stand against antisemitism and support the Jewish people.

Christians United for Israel is committed to making Israel stronger and her people safer. Every day, we work to advocate for Israel and the Jewish people.

Day of Resistance in Columbus, Ohio, on October 12, 2023

Students participating in CUFI's Summit in Washington, D.C., learning how to advocate for Israel on a national stage

Pastor John Hagee addressing CUFI on Campus students, empowering the next generation to support Israel with boldness and faith

Glossary of Terms:

KRISTALLNACHT:
The "Night of Broken Glass" was a state-sponsored pogrom in Nazi Germany that took place on November 9–10, 1938. It was marked by widespread violence against Jews, the destruction of synagogues and businesses, and the arrest of thousands of Jewish men.

NOTES

NOTES

THE WANNSEE CONFERENCE
AND HOLOCAUST
INDUSTRIALIZATION

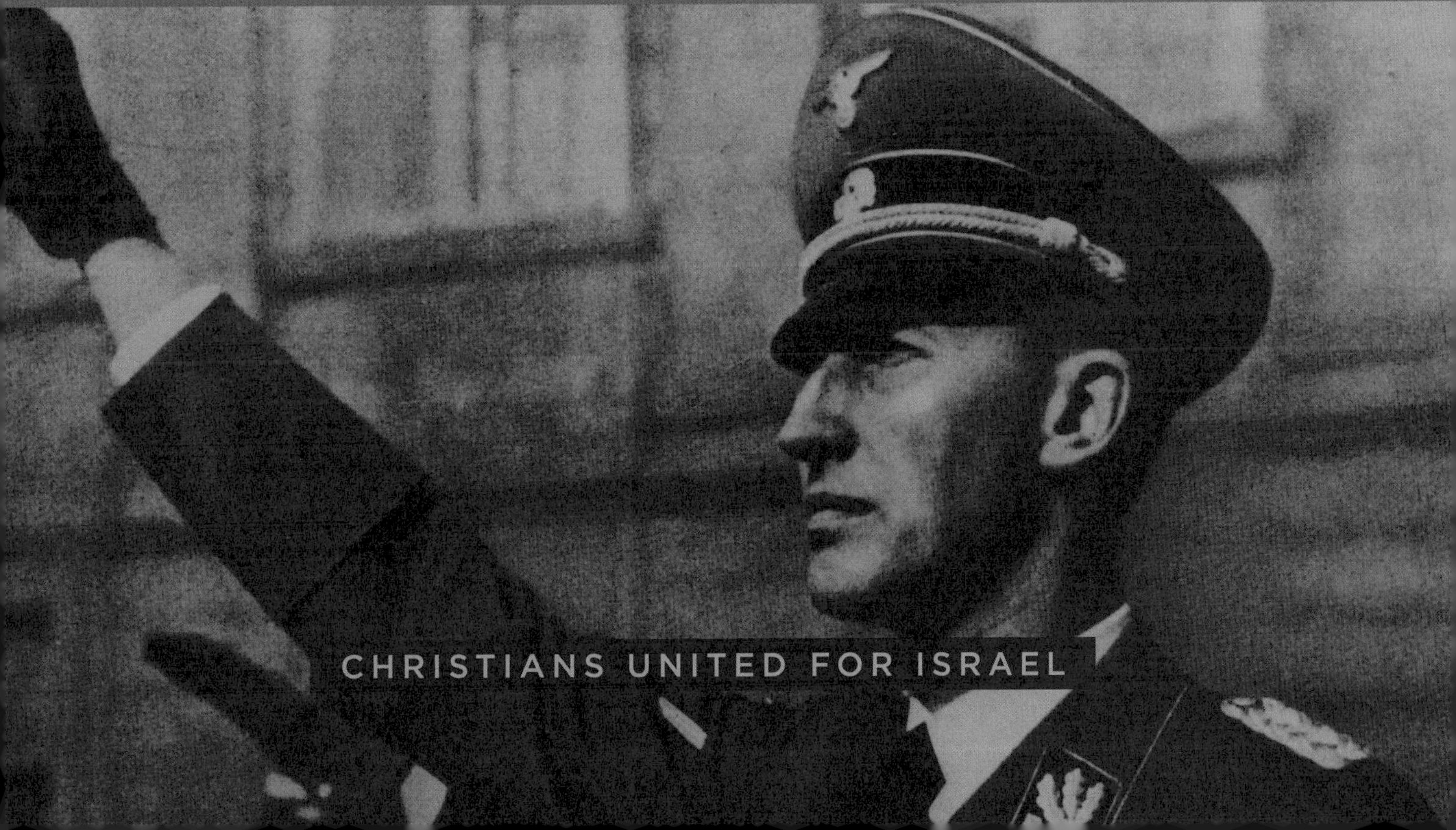

CHRISTIANS UNITED FOR ISRAEL

THE WANNSEE CONFERENCE AND HOLOCAUST INDUSTRIALIZATION

LEARNING OBJECTIVE

In this section, we will explore how the Wannsee Conference formalized the Holocaust's industrialization, analyze the roles of Nazi officials in orchestrating the Final Solution, and reflect on the societal impact of dehumanization and propaganda.

House of the Wannsee Conference

HISTORICAL OVERVIEW

On January 20, 1942, senior Nazi officials gathered at a villa in Wannsee, a Berlin suburb, to formalize the "Final Solution to the Jewish Question." By this time, the Holocaust was already in full motion. However, current methods — though horrific — were deemed inefficient and burdensome by Nazi leadership.

The Wannsee Conference was called to address these "logistical challenges" and unify the Nazi government's approach to genocide. The discussion centered on transforming sporadic killings into a coordinated, industrialized system that could exterminate entire populations more systematically and with fewer resources. This meeting marked a chilling shift in the Holocaust, laying the groundwork for centralized death camps that could kill thousands daily with assembly-line precision.

KEY PARTICIPANTS AND ROLES

Led by SS Obergruppenführer (Major General) Reinhard Heydrich, the Wannsee Conference was the coordination of multiple Nazi offices to officiate a calculated and cold-blooded plan that sought to transform the ongoing mass murder of the Jewish people into a more streamlined and industrial process. They were summoned to Wannsee to work together toward one common goal: the final eradication of all Jews within Nazi-occupied Europe.

REPRESENTATIVE NAZI OFFICES INCLUDED:
Reich Ministry for the Occupied Eastern Territories, Reich Ministry of the Interior, Office of the Plenipotentiary for the Four-Year Plan, Reich Ministry of Justice, Office of the Governor General, Foreign Office, Party Chancellery, Reich Chancellery, SS Race and Settlement Main Office, Reich Security Main Office, Security Police, and Security Service of the SS (SD).

The conference at Wannsee was called in early 1942. However, it was not when mass murder of Jews began. By 1941, mass shootings, mobile gas vans, and the deployment of *Einsatzgruppen* (SS death squads) were already in use, particularly in occupied Eastern Europe.

For instance, the *Einsatzgruppen*, in conjunction with Order Police Battalions, perpetrated the mass shooting of 33,000 Jews at Babi Yar in Ukraine and 25,000 Jews at the Rumbula Forest

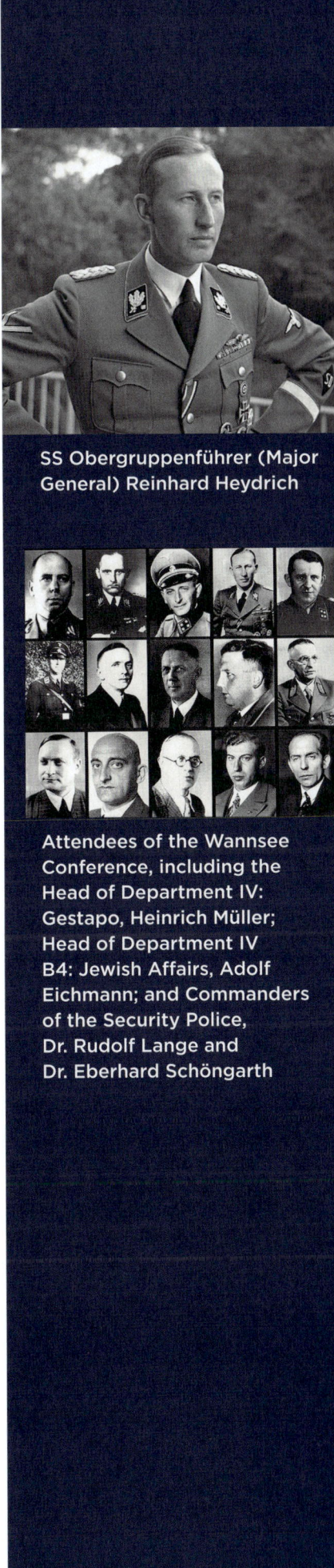

SS Obergruppenführer (Major General) Reinhard Heydrich

Attendees of the Wannsee Conference, including the Head of Department IV: Gestapo, Heinrich Müller; Head of Department IV B4: Jewish Affairs, Adolf Eichmann; and Commanders of the Security Police, Dr. Rudolf Lange and Dr. Eberhard Schöngarth

Interior of a Nazi gas chamber

Auschwitz-Birkenau inmates headed toward the barracks in the camp

Auschwitz-Birkenau concentration camp, 1944

in Latvia. It is estimated that over one million of the six million Jews who died during the Holocaust were murdered in actions and operations such as these — before the Wannsee Conference and the government-wide decision to focus on death camps.

At the time, one of the logistical problems in the eyes of Nazi leadership was that shooting, gas vans, and rounding up large groups of Jews to murder one at a time was largely inefficient. Moreover, it was becoming a burden to the perpetrators.

The Wannsee Conference aimed to restructure the process. The plan would be for all sections of Nazi government to coordinate to transition the killings to a more centralized extermination of the entire population of Jews. Fewer one-on-one shootings, more killing in groups — for example, in large gas chambers where whole groups of Jewish people could be killed with a single container of Zyklon B.

Heinrich Himmler appointed Reinhard Heydrich to oversee the "Final Solution to the Jewish Question." The minutes of the conference (in a document known as the Wannsee Protocol) revealed the regime's systematic approach as the officials discussed the logistics of transporting Jews from across Europe to extermination camps.

⸻

Following the Wannsee Conference, new concentration camps were constructed for the explicit purpose of mass murder, primarily using gas chambers. For example, Auschwitz-Birkenau became a central location, and Treblinka and Sobibor were specifically designed as camps to eradicate as many people as possible, as quickly as possible.

Existing concentration camps were shifted to extermination camps or expanded operations to facilitate the execution of trainload after trainload of Jews.

At the height of Auschwitz operations, the camp's facilities enabled the murder of thousands of people per day — moving an entire group of victims quickly from arrival on a train car, through selection, and into the "shower rooms" all within an hour.

The industrialization of the Holocaust was marked using gas chambers, assembly-line killings, and the exploitation of forced labor. The scale was unprecedented: By the end of WWII, six million Jewish men, women, and children had been murdered.

The Wannsee Conference brought the full weight and power of the Nazi Party into one unified machine regarding the mass murder of the Jewish people. Every element of government was involved. The decisions made that day brought about the mechanization of atrocity.

The results were catastrophic. Though concentration camps were already in use before Wannsee, the plans made at the conference formalized the systematic extermination of all Jews.

TESTIMONIAL CONNECTION

Many Holocaust survivors have borne witness to the horrors they experienced. It is imperative we remember their words and carry their stories on so that future generations may also know what took place.

> "Bergen-Belsen was very different from Auschwitz. In Auschwitz, people were murdered in the most sophisticated manner; in Belsen, they simply perished...We sat about and waited and watched each other deteriorate...The last weeks in Belsen saw the arrival of the death marches from all over Germany. Half-dead people dragged themselves into the compound. They had been marching for days on end and what arrived at the camp were just the remnants. The rest had died on the way." — Anita Lasker-Wallfisch[8]

> "Never shall I forget that night, the first night in camp, that turned my life into one long night, seven times sealed. Never shall I forget that smoke. Never shall I forget the small faces of the children whose bodies I saw transformed into smoke under a silent sky. Never shall I forget those

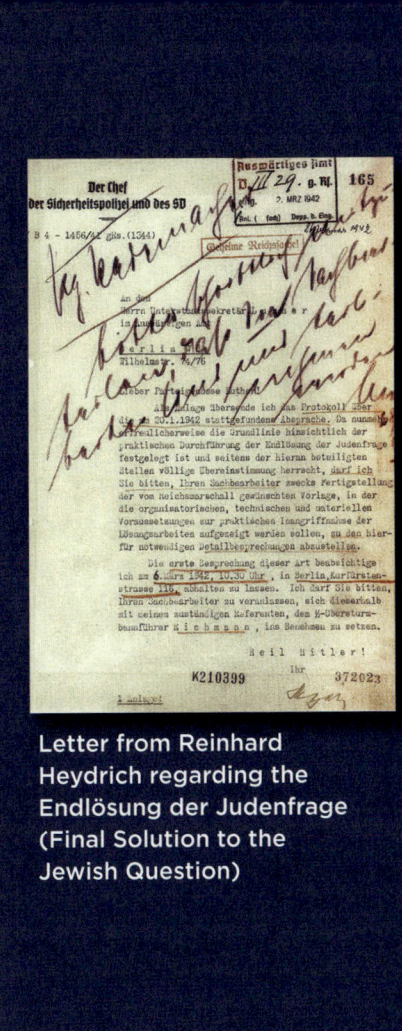

Letter from Reinhard Heydrich regarding the Endlösung der Judenfrage (Final Solution to the Jewish Question)

Bergen-Belsen concentration camp, 1945

Partially excavated mass grave at Bergen-Belsen concentration camp, 1945

Crematorium at Majdanek

Crematorium at Auschwitz

Schutzstaffel propaganda poster for the Nazist military enlistment in Norway, 1942

flames that consumed my faith forever. Never shall I forget that nocturnal silence which deprived me, for all eternity of the desire to live." — Elie Wiesel[9]

What comes to mind when you consider the testimonies of those who survived the Holocaust?

KEY THEMES AND REFLECTION

The Wannsee Conference stands as a reminder of how ideologies of hate can lead to evil, how individuals can commit atrocities. The deportation of entire Jewish communities to concentration camps didn't happen overnight; it was step after step after step.

The Holocaust began with the marginalization of Jews in society, which led to acts of persecution, which escalated to violence. Isolated acts of violence, unchecked and without consequence, snowballed to unimaginable depths of evil.

Those who attended the conference at Wannsee included lawyers, men with doctorates, and high-ranking military members. They were officials and came from educated backgrounds. But each was invited to the table because they oversaw a key element of the Nazi Reich. By day's end, they became the architects of mass genocide.

Real-World Effects of Propaganda

Nazi Party officials, members of the Schutzstaffel (SS) and Sicherheitsdienst (SD), and members of the various offices of the Reich Chancellery had each completely bought into Nazi ideology. The Nazi propaganda ministry achieved its desired result.

Dehumanization

When one group of people believes another group of people are subhuman, it becomes much easier to justify acts of violence upon them.

Antisemitism

The Jewish population were not only stripped of their humanity, but they also bore the brunt of the full weight of the hatred of the Nazi Reich. Antisemitic speeches and policies eventually gave birth to pogroms and death camps.

Appeasement and Indifference

Appeasement grants concessions to aggressive foreign rulers or powers in hopes of avoiding further conflict. Western powers failed to confront the German army's expansion and buildup in Europe in the days leading up to WWII, in effect giving Hitler a free hand to carry out Nazi ideology.

REFLECT:

» How can an educated and cultured society transition into an industrialized regime bent on the genocide of an entire people group?

» What lessons can Christians draw from the Holocaust about the modern-day necessity for continued advocacy for the Jewish people and the need to combat antisemitism in the world today?

INTERACTION EXERCISE

An English translation of the German minutes of the Wannsee Conference is available. It may be viewed here: *Wannsee Protocol*. Spend some time reading the 10-page English translation.

As you read, notice the language used. Words are powerful. The choice of words used within the Wannsee document refers to the extermination of millions of people but uses terminology that dehumanizes and alludes to the same, rather than saying it outright.

» Instead of saying, "deport Jewish civilians on railway cars to death camps," the document says, *"the evacuation of the Jews to the East."* The "East" refers to concentration camps.

Jewish women selected for forced labor at Auschwitz-Birkenau concentration camp

Deportation of Jews to Treblinka

SCAN TO DOWNLOAD WANNSEE PROTOCOL

53

Adolf Eichmann was one of the most pivotal actors in the implementation of the "Final Solution." Charged with managing and facilitating the mass deportation of Jews to ghettos and killing centers in the German-occupied East, he was among the major organizers of the Holocaust.

Heinrich Himmler, IG Farben Auschwitz plant, July 1942

» Instead of saying, "The plan is to murder the entirety of the Jewish population throughout Europe," the document says, *"Approximately 11 million Jews will be involved in the final solution of the European Jewish question."*

» Instead of saying, "The full might of the Nazi war machine is now expected and ordered to work together to mass murder every Jewish man, woman, and child as quickly as possible," the document says, *"The wish of the Reich Marshal to have a draft sent to him concerning organizational, factual and material interests in relation to the final solution of the Jewish question in Europe makes necessary an initial common action of all central offices immediately concerned with these questions in order to bring their general activities into line."*

TEXT STUDY:

EXCERPT 1: *"The most important elements are:*
a) forcing the Jews out of the various spheres of life [Lebensgebiete] of the German people, b) forcing the Jews out of the living space [Lebensraum] of the German people. In pursuit of these endeavours, an intensified and planned effort was made to accelerate the emigration of Jews from the Reich, as the only provisional solution available."

EXCERPT 2: *"In the course of the final solution, and under appropriate supervision, the Jews are to be utilised for work in the East in a suitable manner. In large labour columns, separated by sex, the Jews capable of working will be dispatched to these regions to build roads. In the process, a large portion will undoubtedly drop out through natural reduction."*

ACTIVITY

Read the excerpts from the Protocol and discuss how wording such as *"accelerate the emigration of Jews," "final solution," "in the East,"* and *"natural reduction"* obscures the reality of genocide. How does this sort of detached language reveal the worldview of the Nazi regime regarding Jewish people?

GROUP DISCUSSION

In what ways do you see how society today has become detached from compassion for people in need, the horror of murder, antisemitic riots, and a lack of a moral compass? Is industrialized genocide possible again?

ENGAGE FURTHER

Watch this video to uncover how key Nazi leaders orchestrated a horrific plan aiming to annihilate the Jewish population and leading to the tragic loss of millions of lives. What does this reveal about the consequences of hatred left unchecked?

REFLECTION AND ACTION

The meeting of 15 officials of the Wannsee Conference was conducted in an orderly fashion and overseen by educated men. They were senior government officials who aimed to "cleanse German living space of Jews by legal means." The meeting took place in a beautiful villa, and brandy and cigars were at hand afterwards. In the context of luxury, the genocide of millions was planned.

The meeting did not take place in a vacuum. The systematic destruction and plan for the genocide of European Jewry was already an established Nazi policy. Jews had been subjected to persecution and death for years. However, the purpose of Wannsee was to outline how the Nazi Reich could coordinate a unified effort to eradicate the Jewish population as efficiently as possible.

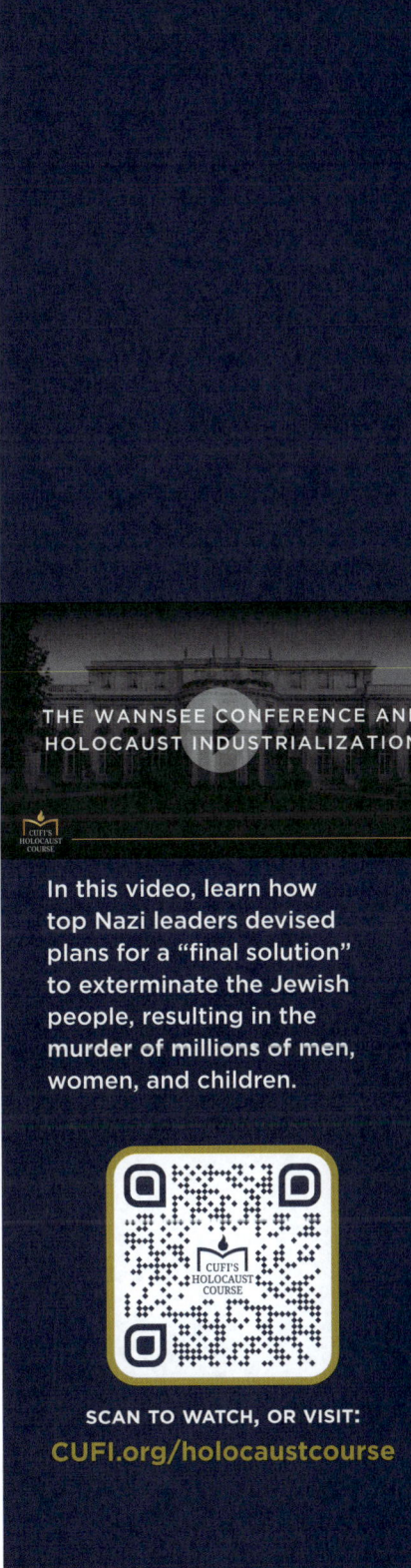

THE WANNSEE CONFERENCE AND HOLOCAUST INDUSTRIALIZATION

In this video, learn how top Nazi leaders devised plans for a "final solution" to exterminate the Jewish people, resulting in the murder of millions of men, women, and children.

SCAN TO WATCH, OR VISIT:
CUFI.org/holocaustcourse

Shoes of victims at Auschwitz concentration camp

The Wannsee Conference reveals the devastating consequences of dehumanization, of antisemitism, of the power of racial ideologies, and of the capabilities of the depths of evil.

By the time the 15 attendees of the conference sat down around a table to meet, a Jew was no longer a person in their minds, but rather a problem that needed a "solution."

We must learn the stories of the past, consider the impacts of the rule of evil left to its own devices, and seek how we may act, advocate, and engage with the immediate defense of Israel and the Jewish people.

> » How can you actively combat antisemitism in your community or circle of influence?
> » What opportunities might you have to educate others about the Holocaust and advocate for the Jewish people?

Aerial view of Auschwitz

Glossary of Terms:

SCHUTZSTAFFEL (SS):
A Nazi Party paramilitary group that became one of the most powerful elements within the Nazi regime. Various units within the SS included death squads, concentration camp officials, the Gestapo, and enforcers of Nazi racial policy.

SICHERHEITSDIENST (SD):
The intelligence agency of the SS in Nazi Germany. Operations included expanded surveillance on individuals or organizations considered a threat to the Nazi Reich as well as enforcing Nazi ideology.

WANNSEE CONFERENCE:
A meeting held on January 20, 1942, in Berlin, Germany, in the locality of Wannsee. Fifteen Nazi Party officials attended, and plans were formalized to organize the entirety of the Nazi Reich for the destruction of all European Jewry.

WANNSEE PROTOCOL:
The official record of the Wannsee Conference. The document outlined the coordinated plan for the "Final Solution to the Jewish Question," the systematic extermination of the entire Jewish population under Nazi rule.

NOTES

NOTES

"Never shall I forget those flames that consumed my faith forever. Never shall I forget that nocturnal silence which deprived me, for all eternity of the desire to live."

ELIE WIESEL

RESISTANCE AND
STORIES OF SURVIVAL

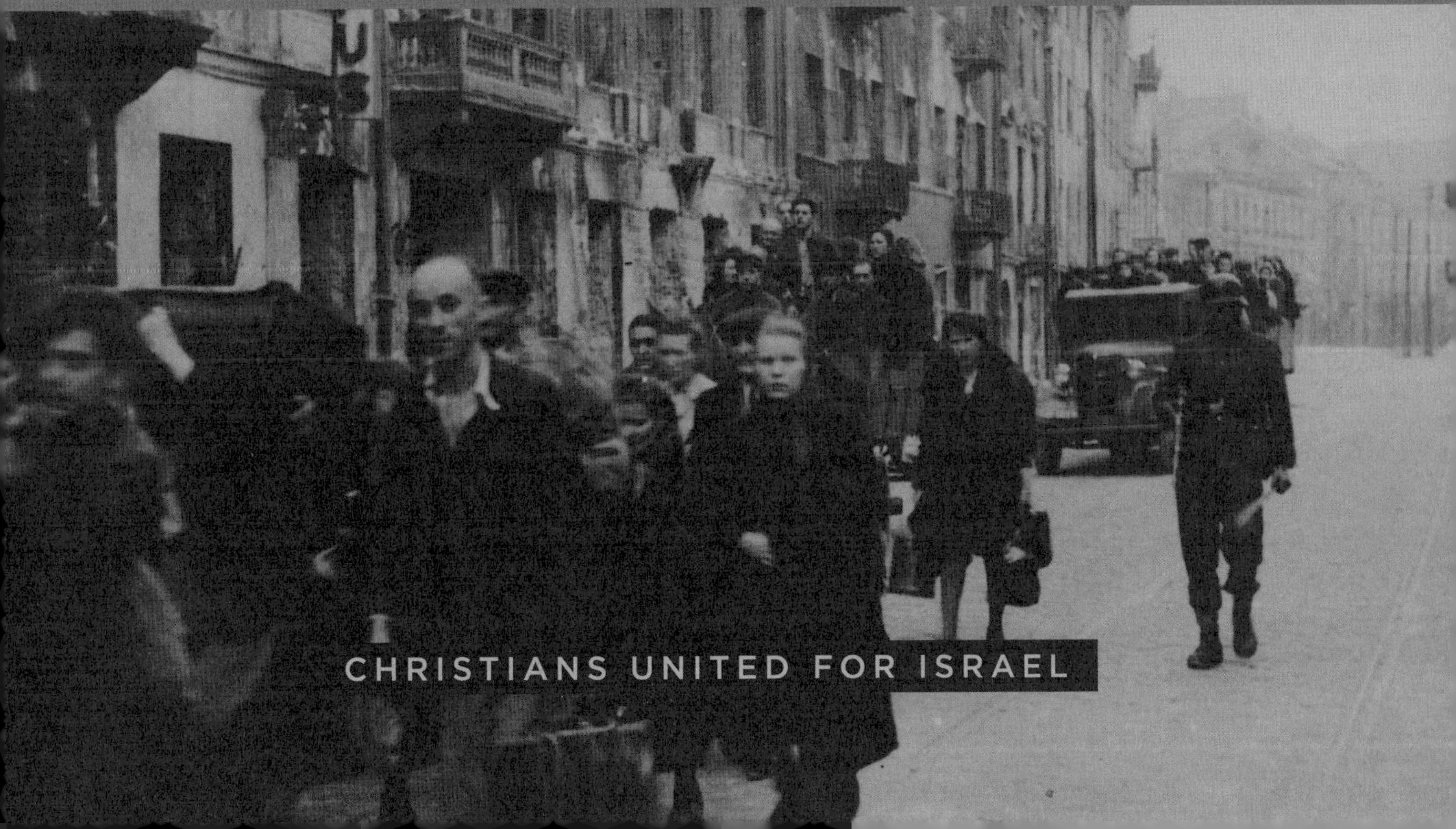

CHRISTIANS UNITED FOR ISRAEL

RESISTANCE AND STORIES OF SURVIVAL

LEARNING OBJECTIVE

In this section, we will highlight the courageous acts of resistance and the extraordinary resilience of individuals who stood against Nazi genocide during the Holocaust, exploring their enduring legacy of hope and defiance. Against all odds, men, women, and children defied the fear of certain death and fought for freedom and life.

Nazi soldiers cutting off the beard of an Orthodox Jew

HISTORICAL OVERVIEW

As Adolf Hitler's Nazi war machine stormed across Europe, Jewish people across the continent faced the horrors of industrialized, mechanized, and weaponized evil.

Their communities faced systematic persecution and the threat of annihilation as the Nazi regime sought to erase their presence from history, one life at a time. Before the war's end, six million Jews would be murdered.

And yet, despite the overwhelming odds and the unimaginable cruelty inflicted upon them, story after story after story would soon surface of how many fought back in any and every way possible. Though many lost their lives in this dark period of history, the Jewish people displayed remarkable acts of courage.

Against the backdrop of indescribable suffering, pain, and heartbreak, heroic stories of defiance and resistance shine through the pages of history as beacons of hope and sources of light during this dark and evil period. Their stories are a testament to the resilience of the Jewish spirit and the enduring power of faith and hope, even in the valley of the shadow of death.

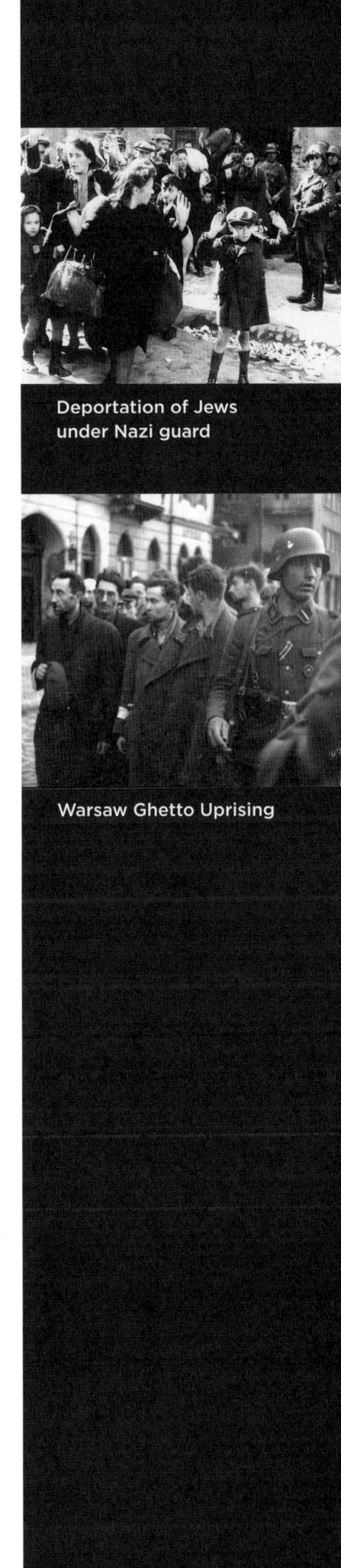

Deportation of Jews under Nazi guard

Warsaw Ghetto Uprising

RESISTANCE

Resistance often took the form of small, under-equipped groups engaging in covert guerrilla warfare, while others organized large-scale uprisings or preserved vital cultural artifacts.

From smuggling food and medicine into ghettos to preserving sacred Torah scrolls to documenting the atrocities in diaries and letters, every measure, no matter how small, was powerful. Through every heroic and courageous act, the world knows today how people stood up to tyranny and fought back against evil.

SURVIVAL

Surviving the Holocaust required a stubborn will to live, extraordinary resourcefulness, and unshakeable faith. Despite the efforts of the entire power of the Nazi Reich devoted to the destruction of the Jewish people, many survived the war.

The courage, resilience, and hope of those imprisoned in concentration camps stand as a profound testament to the unyielding strength of the human spirit, even amidst unimaginable suffering. Their stories must never be forgotten. They challenge us to continue to fight against evil with both word and deed.

Jewish resistance fighters arrested during the liquidation of the Warsaw Ghetto

The burning of the Warsaw Ghetto

Families evaded capture in countless ways including hiding in attics and basements and even living in forests through harsh weather and winter. Many were aided by brave non-Jews, both neighbors and complete strangers, who risked their own lives to save them. Survival, in many cases, depended on working together with others and never giving up hope.

Survivors of concentration camps endured unimaginable horrors yet chose to rebuild their lives after the war, stepping fully into newfound freedom. They faced hell on earth yet persevered to a bright future. They would live to have families, build businesses, and positively impact their communities. Those who resisted and those who survived remind us that hope can be found even in the darkest times. Their stories emphasize the importance of standing firm in faith, supporting those in need, and never giving up.

THE WARSAW GHETTO UPRISING

One of the largest and most well-known acts of resistance is the Warsaw Ghetto Uprising. The Warsaw ghetto, established in 1940, was the largest Jewish ghetto throughout occupied Europe. Approximately 400,000 Jews were crammed into a 1.3 square mile area with an average of nine people per room.

In 1942, German SS and police units began what was known as the "Great Action." Disguised as a resettlement program, this was, in fact, a mass deportation of the Warsaw ghetto population to Treblinka, one of the most notorious Nazi extermination camps. By early 1943, approximately 70,000 to 80,000 Jews were left within the ghetto.

Those who survived the "Great Action" realized their impending fate. Two key groups organized within the ghetto to fight back: the Jewish Combat Organization (*Żydowska Organizacja Bojowa*; ŻOB) and a secondary force called the Jewish Military Union (*Żydowski Związek Wojskowy*; ŻZW). With a strength of just 750 people total, they secured what weapons they could from the Polish underground and prepared to fight for their lives.

On April 19, 1943, the Warsaw Ghetto Uprising began with courageous Jewish fighters employing guerrilla tactics, wielding pistols, homemade grenades, and a few automatic weapons against overwhelming Nazi forces. The initial surprise attack was successful, killing a dozen Nazis and forcing the German troops to retreat.

The Nazis reorganized with artillery, tanks, and a force of over 2,000 soldiers and police. The uprising lasted 27 days. In the end, the Warsaw ghetto was torched and razed to the ground.

THE BIELSKI PARTISANS

Another significant resistance effort was that of the Bielski Partisans. Named after three brothers who led the group, they became one of the largest resistance operations of the war.

After their parents were murdered in December of 1941, Tuvia, Asael, and Zus Bielski decided to flee to the forests to survive. There they established a partisan detachment of Jewish families. Through non-Jewish Belorussian contacts, they began to acquire guns and later added captured German and Soviet munitions to their arsenal. They waged guerrilla-style warfare, disabling Nazi-held trains, railroads, and bridges, and attacking patrols.

Committed to saving and protecting as many lives as possible, they rescued Jews from ghettos, protected escapees on the roads, and welcomed every Jew, no matter their age or gender, if they were sick and infirm, into their ranks.

Deep within the forests, the "Bielski otriad" established a community, complete with tailors, carpenters, cobblers, and blacksmiths. They constructed a mill, bakery, school, and synagogue. Tuvia believed to save one Jew was of greater importance than to kill twenty Germans. When the Soviet Army liberated Belorussia in the summer of 1944, the Bielski group was 1,200 strong, most of whom would not have survived the war alone.

Deportation of Jews during the Warsaw Ghetto Uprising

Members of the Bielski Partisans in the Naliboki Forest
(United States Holocaust Memorial Museum Photo Archives)

Tuvia Bielski
(United States Holocaust Memorial Museum Photo Archives)

Anne Frank (1929–1945)

Anne Frank's diary

Het Achterhuis by Anne Frank

TESTIMONIAL CONNECTION

Remembering the Jewish girl who documented her life in hiding from the Nazis during World War II

Anne Frank was born in Frankfurt, Germany, in 1929. The Frank family was Jewish and began to feel the immediate impacts and threats of Jewish persecution and rampant antisemitism in Germany. To escape, the Franks emigrated to the Netherlands in 1934.

However, in May of 1940, the Dutch army surrendered to the German army, and the Netherlands fell under Nazi occupation. Freedom for every Jew under Nazi rule in their hometown of Amsterdam eroded away. Seemingly overnight, Jews could no longer visit parks or cinemas. Anne was forced to go to a separate, Jewish-only school, and her father, Otto, was forbidden from continuing to run his business.

Jews were forced to wear a Star of David in public as rumors of deportation filled the streets. When Anne's sister, Margot, received a call with instructions to report to a "labor camp," the family went into hiding in the annex of Otto's business at Prinsengracht 263.

The Frank family and a few others hid in this secret space for over two years. Anne would keep a diary, writing about her life, emotions, and thoughts as a young teenage girl in hiding. One day she heard a report on Radio Orange from the Minister of Education of the Dutch government. The call was to preserve wartime diaries and documents. Anne began to compile her writings into one document called *Het Achterhuis* (*The Secret Annex*).

On August 4th, 1944, the annex was raided by German police. Anne's family was deported to Auschwitz-Birkenau. They travelled in a cattle car, packed together with 1,000 other Jews on a three-day journey. In November of 1944, Anne and her sister Margot were transferred to Bergen-Belsen. They both contracted typhus and died in February of 1945.

Anne's father, Otto, was liberated from Auschwitz by Soviet troops and was the sole survivor of his family. He published Anne's diary in June of 1947, with a first printing of 3,000 copies. Her story quickly became known worldwide. *Het Achterhuis* was translated into 70 languages, as well as adaptations for stage and film. In 1960, the hiding place became a museum, the Anne Frank House. Otto continued telling Anne's story and remained involved with the museum for the rest of his life.

The story of Anne Frank is now globally known. Why is her life so compelling? What about the diary of a teenager living in hiding has captivated the thoughts and imaginations of millions of people?

KEY THEMES AND REFLECTION

Throughout the pages of history and around the world, generation after generation has tried to eradicate the Jewish people. But none have ever been able to do so. Below is a non-comprehensive list of tragedies that have befallen the Jewish people at the hands of evil empires, regimes, and movements:

1. Slavery in Egypt: 400 years in slavery before the Exodus
2. Assyrian Empire: conquest of the Northern Kingdom of Israel (722 BC)
3. Babylonian Empire: conquest of Judah and destruction of the First Temple by Nebuchadnezzar and Jews exiled to Babylon (586 BC)
4. Seleucid Empire: suppression of Jewish practices during the 2nd century BC and attempted forced Hellenization, sparking the Maccabean Revolt (167–160 BC)
5. Roman Empire: destruction of the Second Temple in 70 AD before the Jewish revolt and the Bar Kokhba Revolt (132–135 AD), marking the beginning of the Jewish Diaspora
6. Byzantine Empire: imposition of anti-Jewish laws (particularly harsh from the 4th–7th centuries)

Passageway to the secret annex

Anne Frank in 1942

Jewish women and children, some wearing Nazi designated yellow stars, arrive by rail to Auschwitz-Birkenau concentration camp

Intifada in the Gaza Strip

7. Visigoth Empire: forced conversion of Jews in Spain in the 6th and 7th centuries, converted Jews labeled "conversos"

8. Islamic Caliphates: forced conversion to Islam, forced life as a *dhimmi* (non-Muslim with lower status), or expulsion from Muslim lands

9. Crusader States: massacres of Jewish populations from 11th–13th centuries

10. Medieval European Kingdoms: continual expulsions or massacres of Jewish communities

11. Spanish Inquisition: 1478–1834 in Spain including forced expulsions or conversions

12. Russian Empire: late 18th century, Jews in Russia targeted by economic persecution and violent pogroms

13. Nazi Germany: 1933–1945, over six million Jews killed in the Holocaust

14. Soviet Union: suppression of Jewish practice and life, especially during the Cold War

15. Modern-day Islamic Terrorist Organizations: continual terror attacks against Israel and Jewish people

Though empires, armies, and nations have sought to destroy the Jewish people, one by one, these powers have faded into history while the Jewish people remain. Nothing on earth has been able to extinguish the enduring flame of the Jewish people.

Read

Thus says the LORD,
Who gives the sun for a light by day,
The ordinances of the moon and the stars for a light by night,
Who disturbs the sea, and its waves roar
(The LORD of hosts is His name):
"If those ordinances depart from before Me," says the LORD,
"Then the seed of Israel shall also cease
From being a nation before Me forever."
Thus says the LORD:
"If heaven above can be measured,

And the foundations of the earth searched out beneath,
I will also cast off all the seed of Israel
For all that they have done, says the LORD."
JEREMIAH 31:35–37 (NKJV)

Relief of the inner panel of the Arch of Titus in Rome, Italy, which displays Roman soldiers carrying off spoils including a menorah after the destruction of Jerusalem in 70 AD

Consider

What does Jeremiah 31 say about the Jewish people specifically? If God has declared that they will never cease to be a nation before Him, how does that help us understand how, no matter how forcefully powers have tried to destroy them, the Jewish people have continually survived throughout history?

INTERACTION EXERCISE

Exploring the real-life stories of Holocaust resistance and survival inspires us to reflect on our own lives and the actions we can take to stand against injustice today. For Christians who support Israel, these stories are a reminder that evil has and will continue to seek to raise its head. Antisemitism has never faded from history. Indifference, apathy, and lack of action, when action was necessary, only emboldened evil to continue to march across the earth.

The Warsaw Ghetto Uprising

ENGAGE FURTHER

Be part of CUFI's mission by attending an event near you. Attend a local Night to Honor Israel, participate in a CUFI on Campus event, or explore our online resources to deepen your knowledge of Israel's history and significance. https://cufi.org/cufi-events/

Study

Reflect on the testimony of a Holocaust survivor. What can you learn from their experiences, and how can their resilience and courage shape the way you approach challenges in your own life?

Jewish men mounting a Nazi Germany lorry from the ghettos of Warsaw, Poland

Prisoners at Auschwitz-Birkenau concentration camp

RESISTANCE AND STORIES OF SURVIVAL

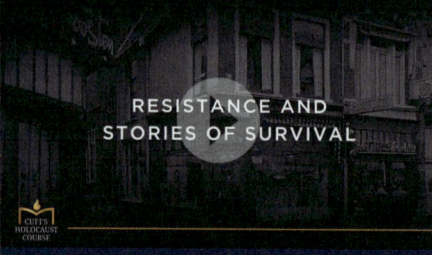

Hear about courageous non-Jews who refused to remain silent in the face of evil, risking their own lives by helping their Jewish neighbors.

SCAN TO WATCH, OR VISIT:
CUFI.org/holocaustcourse

Consider

Journal to yourself or discuss with a group:

> » What was the underlying motivation of individuals and groups to resist against overwhelming odds? What would be your motivation?
>
> » How does the power of faith and community with others factor into survival during a war?
>
> » What lessons can we apply to our own lives today regarding supporting Israel, combatting antisemitism, or standing up for what is right?

GO FURTHER

A single story or testimony holds great weight. **Watch the video** and consider the life of someone who lived, died, or survived through WWII. Let this account bring history to life for you and inspire you to draw near to God yourself and fulfill His purpose and plan for you.

REFLECTION AND ACTION

The ten Boom family was a family of deep conviction and faith. They believed living out their faith meant that they would not back down or appease evil, even under threat of imprisonment or death. As Christians, we are called to love our neighbor and to stand with the Jewish people. The ten Boom family's unwavering faith and courage demonstrate the transformative power of standing against evil, even when it demands profound sacrifice.

CORRIE TEN BOOM

The ten Boom family lived in the Netherlands. They were deeply devoted Christians who were also ardent supporters of the Jewish people. Corrie grew up in a family that loved God, was devoted to prayer, and held firmly to deep religious beliefs and convictions. Her grandfather, Willem ten

Boom, started a weekly prayer service to pray for the Jewish people and the peace of Jerusalem in 1844.

Corrie's father, Casper ten Boom, continued the tradition, and Corrie and her sister grew up in a home committed to the tradition of prayer. Unfortunately, the family prayer meetings ended when Nazi soldiers arrested the entire ten Boom family for harboring Jews.

During the war and under Nazi occupation, the ten Boom family used their home as a refuge for hiding Jews. Their cover was the family-owned store, a watchmaking and repair shop. They became an integral part of the underground Dutch resistance, hiding Jews in a secret room in their home in Haarlem and helping Jews connect with other safe houses.

On February 28, 1944, the Gestapo raided the house. Six Jews and resistance workers who were in the hiding place were not discovered, but the Gestapo arrested 30 people who were in the home that day. Her father died in the penitentiary in Scheveningen, and her sister died at Ravensbrück concentration camp.

It is estimated that the ten Booms saved as many as 800 Jews during the war, as well as many Dutch underground resistance members. For her part in saving so many lives, Corrie ten Boom was recognized as one of the "Righteous Among the Nations" by the Yad Vashem Remembrance Authority on December 12, 1967.

Holocaust survivors from Nazi oppression in WWII

Corrie ten Boom in her family shop in Haarlem

Passage to the ten Boom's hiding place

Avenue of "Righteous Among the Nations" at Yad Vashem Holocaust Museum in Jerusalem, Israel

REFLECT

What did it cost the ten Boom family to join the Dutch resistance? Why did they do what they did, even though it meant they could be arrested?

ACT

Attend a CUFI event that supports the Jewish people in your city. You could also organize an event at your school, church, or university that tells the stories of Jewish people who resisted Nazi occupation during WWII.

PRAY

Willem ten Boom started a weekly prayer service for his family to pray for the Jewish people and the peace of Jerusalem. Those prayers changed the course of his entire family tree, changed the trajectory of his son and granddaughters' lives, and saved hundreds of people during a world war. What if you started a weekly prayer meeting to pray for the Jewish people and the peace of Jerusalem as well? Who knows what impact it may one day make?

The ten Boom family shop in Haarlem, Netherlands, 1961

Glossary of Terms:

BIELSKI PARTISANS:
A Jewish resistance group in Belarus during World War II. Led by the Bielski brothers, they saved over 1,200 Jews while fighting Nazis with guerrilla tactics and offering a safe haven to any Jew they found.

DIARY OF ANNE FRANK:
The journal of Anne Frank, a Jewish teenager who hid for two years in Amsterdam while the Netherlands were under Nazi occupation. It captures her thoughts, hopes, and dreams and became a key historical document from the Holocaust.

WARSAW GHETTO UPRISING:
A 1943 Jewish revolt against Nazi efforts to deport ghetto residents to death camps in Warsaw, Poland. Despite being outmatched, the fighters resisted for 27 days, symbolizing defiance during the Holocaust.

ŻYDOWSKA ORGANIZACJA BOJOWA; ŻOB:
The Jewish Combat Organization, a Jewish resistance group in Nazi-occupied Poland. It fought during the Warsaw Ghetto Uprising in 1943, aiming to resist deportations and fight Nazi oppression.

ŻYDOWSKI ZWIĄZEK WOJSKOWY; ŻZW:
The Jewish Military Union, a Jewish underground military group formed by former Polish officers. They collaborated with the ŻOB to fight in the Warsaw Ghetto Uprising.

NOTES

NOTES

"I keep my ideals, because in spite of everything I still believe that people are really good at heart."

ANNE FRANK, FROM
THE DIARY OF A YOUNG GIRL

POST-WWII
LIBERATION STRUGGLES

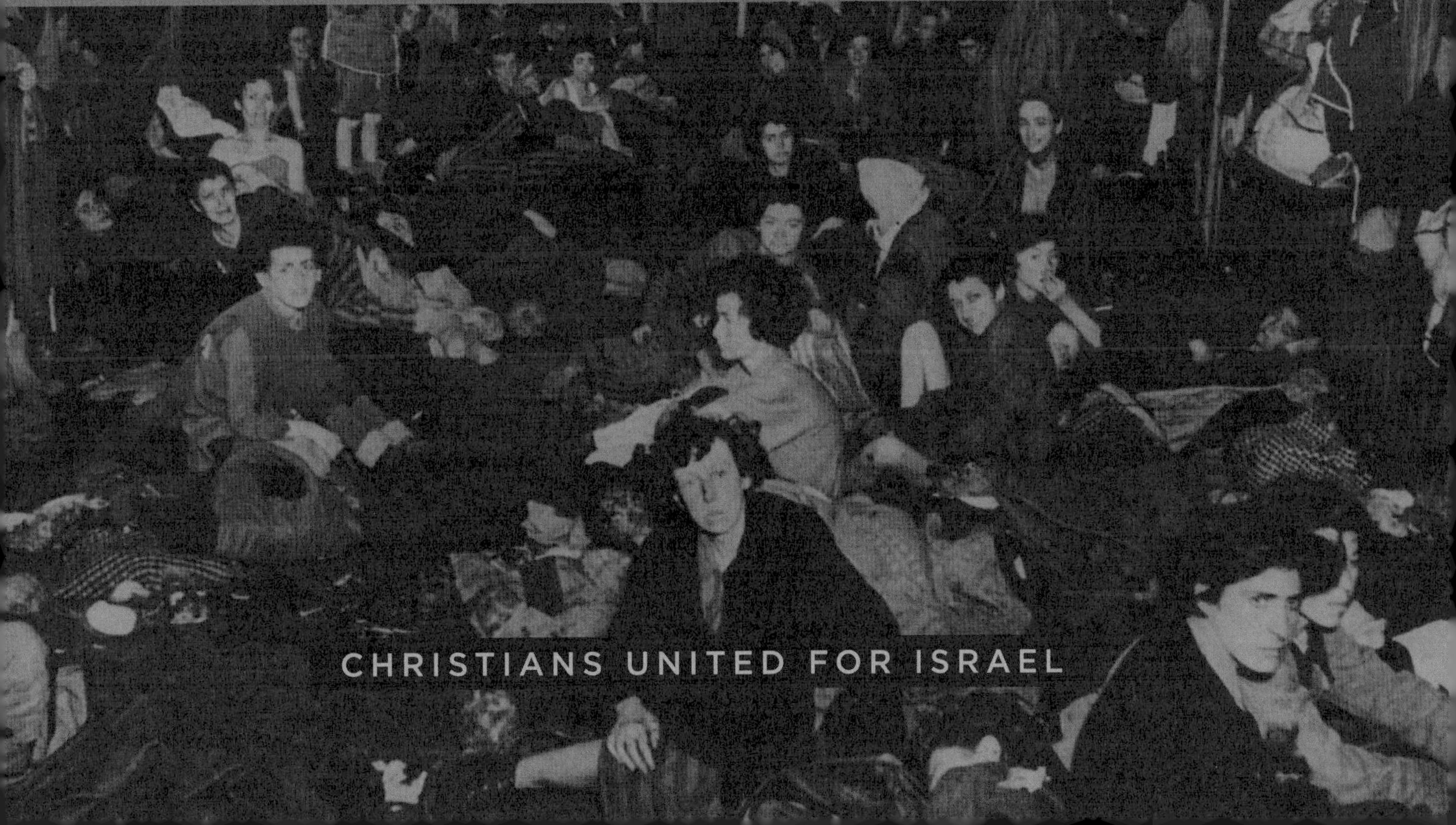

POST-WWII LIBERATION STRUGGLES

LEARNING OBJECTIVE

In this section, we will explore what life was like for the Jewish people in the immediate aftermath of the Holocaust. We will examine their struggles in the period directly after WWII, including the challenges faced by survivors and the continual resilience of the Jewish people.

Jewish civilians with raised hands during a Nazi roundup, marked by the yellow Star of David they were forced to wear at all times

HISTORICAL OVERVIEW

The Jewish people's survival of the Holocaust's systematic extermination stands as a profound testament to their resilience. For millennia, the children of Israel had been chased, abused, othered, and murdered. The horrors of World War II left six million Jews murdered, survivors displaced and often alone, and entire communities shattered, broken, and destitute.

Yet, against this backdrop of a tragic history and this unspeakable loss, the Jewish people began a remarkable journey of restoration and renewal into a new reality of life and hope in a post-war world.

DISPLACED PERSONS CAMPS

Victory in Europe Day was May 8, 1945. That day marked the end of WWII and the beginning of a new era. However, at war's end, millions of people in Europe had been displaced. Many of those who survived the Holocaust sought to leave Europe forever but could not do so due to restrictive immigration policies by other countries. Therefore, hundreds of thousands of Holocaust survivors found themselves stuck in Europe and found shelter in "Displaced Persons Camps" set up by the Allies.

Displaced persons (DP) camps were often established in former concentration camps or military barracks, where resources were scarce, overcrowding was severe, and medical care was limited. Survivors faced the overwhelming challenge of rebuilding their lives in conditions that mirrored imprisonment. Remarkably, weddings and births were common in DP camps. The creation of the State of Israel in May of 1948 and the passing of the United States Displaced Persons Act of June 1948 allowed the emigration of many former camp residents to America and Israel.

THE JEWISH RELIEF UNIT

Many relief organizations operated to address the needs of Holocaust survivors after WWII. One of them was the Jewish Relief Unit (JRU), which was active from 1945 to 1950. As part of the Jewish Committee for Relief Abroad, its focus was to bring relief and aid to Jews living in Europe. The unit worked closely within DP camps, helping survivors acquire identity documents as well as attempting to locate and reunite families. The JRU provided child welfare clinics, as well as medical aid and assistance for those in need.

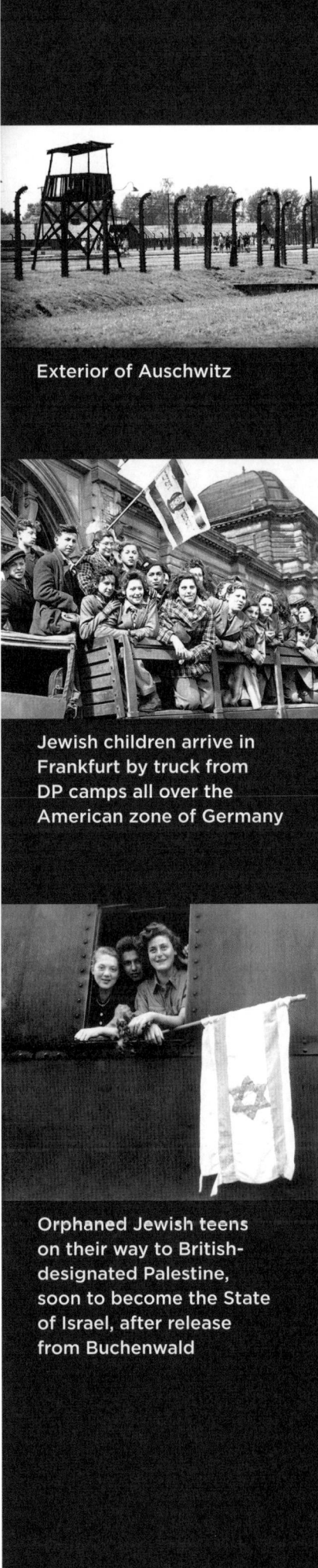

Exterior of Auschwitz

Jewish children arrive in Frankfurt by truck from DP camps all over the American zone of Germany

Orphaned Jewish teens on their way to British-designated Palestine, soon to become the State of Israel, after release from Buchenwald

THE KIELCE POGROM

Despite the end of the Holocaust, antisemitism persisted in Europe, creating additional challenges for survivors. Though the war was over, hatred against the Jewish people was still very real in the hearts and minds of millions of people. The Kielce pogrom was one of the first pogroms that claimed Jewish lives after the end of WWII. It took place on July 4, 1946, in Kielce, Poland. The pogrom began because a 9-year-old boy was reported missing. Upon his return, his father claimed the boy had been kidnapped and held in the cellar of a house.

The house was the "Jewish House" at 7 Planty Street, which had become the refuge of Jewish survivors of the Holocaust who had returned to Poland. (The boy later redacted his story in an interview in 1998.) After news of the kidnapping was reported and the Citizens Militia was informed, the group dispatched an armed patrol to the house to investigate. They published the blood libel story that they were searching for other non-Jewish children who were "ritually murdered by the Jews" at the house. Escalation of violence ensued, and in the end, 42 Jewish men, women, and children were killed, many beaten to death. Incidents like these pushed many Jews to leave Europe altogether, fueling emigration to places like the United States, Israel, and South America.

BRITISH WHITE PAPER OF 1939

The British Mandate for Palestine lasted from 1920 to 1948, during which time the land was under British administration, and the British government issued the White Paper of 1939. That white paper became a significantly important British governing policy document regarding the administration of Palestine and subsequently impacted Jewish emigration.

The White Paper limited Jewish immigration to 75,000 people during the years of WWII, between 1940 and 1945. It also imposed strict land restrictions on Jewish purchases and proposed the establishment of Palestine as jointly governed by Jews and Arabs,

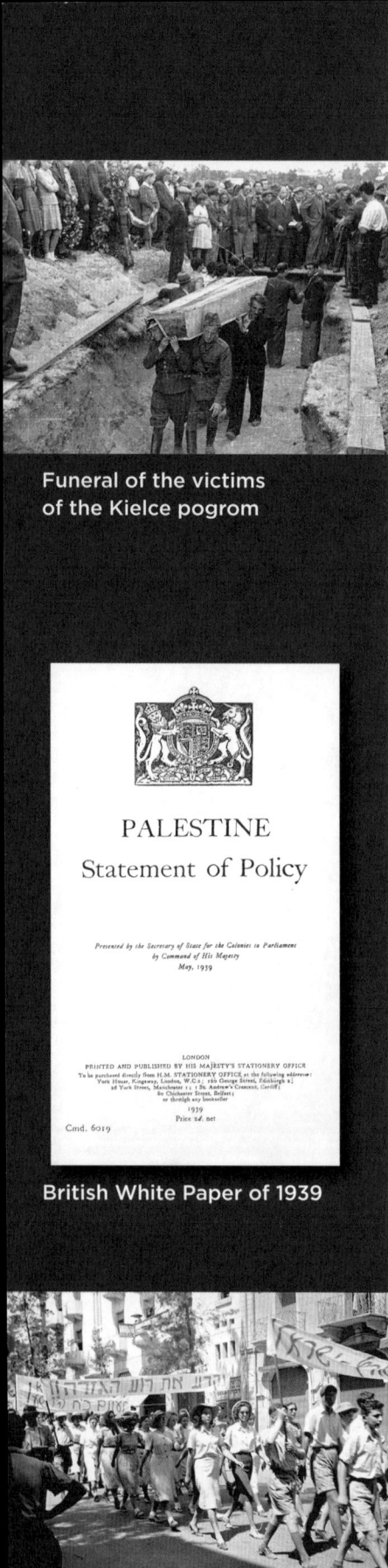

Funeral of the victims of the Kielce pogrom

British White Paper of 1939

Jewish protest demonstrations in Jerusalem against the British White Paper, May 18, 1939

effectively reneging on the Balfour Declaration of 1917 and wiping out the possibility of a sovereign Jewish state. Immigration of Jews beyond the 75,000 mark required Arab consent. The document effectively kept millions of Jews in Europe during the period of the Holocaust as well as restricted them from emigrating to Israel after WWII.

Theodor Herzl

REBUILDING JEWISH CULTURE

Liberation brought freedom but also immense psychological and physical challenges. Survivors suffered from malnutrition, illness, and post-traumatic stress. Many grappled with guilt, grief, and life-long pain. The transition to life outside concentration camps was often fraught with difficulty, as survivors struggled to reclaim their humanity in a world that had changed.

After the Holocaust, Jewish survivors sought to revive Jewish culture and traditions that the Nazis had tried to eradicate. Educational programs, religious services, and community events became vital ways of reconnecting to Jewish heritage. For example, Yiddish and Hebrew literature, art, and music flourished as a means to express identity, and great efforts were made across the Jewish world to set up Holocaust memorials, Jewish cultural institutions, and continual building of Jewish youth movements.

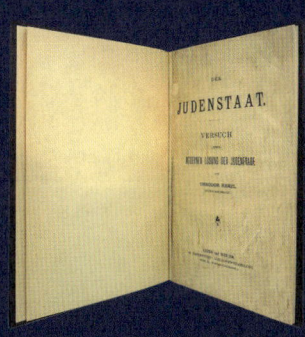

Der Judenstaat (The Jewish State), a book by Theodor Herzl, making the case for the need of a sovereign Jewish homeland to avoid antisemitism in Europe; published in 1896

TESTIMONIAL CONNECTION

Irving Roth was born in 1929 into a Jewish family in Czechoslovakia. As a teenager, his life was forever changed by the rise of Nazi Germany and the horrors of the Holocaust. He and his brother were sent to Auschwitz, where Irving survived brutal conditions, the death of his brother, and the forced marches to Buchenwald. When Buchenwald was liberated in April of 1945, Irving was finally free but had no idea what had become of his family.

Irving Roth, of blessed memory, was a Holocaust survivor and educator whose life and work inspired countless individuals to remember and learn from the horrors of the Holocaust

Russian displaced persons and former prisoners leaving camps near Hamburg, May 31, 1945

Jewish displaced persons receive bread rations at the Bindermichl DP camp in Linz

Displaced persons and refugees in Germany, May 18, 1945

With the war over, Irving made the long and uncertain journey back to his hometown, unsure of what awaited him. He found both his mother and father alive. His parents had survived by hiding in Hungary, thanks to the bravery and compassion of a local family who risked their lives to protect them. Finding any family alive was uncommon for Jews in Europe after the war, so for a survivor who had endured unimaginable loss and suffering, this reunion was nothing short of miraculous.

Irving's reunion with his parents was not just a personal victory but a symbol of the perseverance and strength that defines those who endured the Holocaust.

What does this story of Irving's reunion with his parents teach you about the power of hope and the ability to find light in the darkest of times?

KEY THEMES AND REFLECTION

The post-WWII era stands as a defining moment in Jewish history. Six million Jewish lives were lost, entire communities obliterated, and survivors faced the immense challenge of rebuilding their lives in a world devoid of a Jewish homeland.

Tikkun Olam

One of the key concepts in Jewish tradition and life is "*Tikkun Olam*" (תיקון עולם), a Hebrew phrase that means "Repair the world." After World War II, *Tikkun Olam* once again became a central guiding concept in Jewish efforts to rebuild communities, promote justice, and heal from tragedy. It helped guide the Jewish people toward the establishment of the State of Israel and continued to inspire global Jewish humanitarian work, Holocaust education, and activism.

Nuremberg trial, 1946

The Nuremberg Trials

The Nuremberg Trials were a series of military tribunals held by the International Military Tribunal of members of the Allies and took place from 1945 to 1946. The purpose of the trials was to prosecute key Nazi officials and leaders who participated in war crimes, genocide, use of forced labor, and crimes against humanity during the Holocaust. The trials held Nazi perpetrators and conspirators accountable for their actions, even sentencing multiple defendants to death by hanging. The trials executed justice upon those responsible for evil and were a testimony of the world's commitment to prosecute evil and remember the Holocaust.

REFLECT:

» How do you think the concept of *Tikkun Olam* helped shape Jewish life after WWII?

» The Jewish people watched the world hold the Nuremberg Trials. In what ways did they serve justice or act as a balm on the wounds of Holocaust survivors?

Rudolf Hess and other leaders of the Nazi Party at the Nuremberg Trials

Photojournalists waiting for high-ranking Nazis to exit the Nuremberg Trials courtroom

1945: *The Daily Telegraph* front page reporting trial of Vidkun Quisling

Liberation of Holland,
May 7, 1945

Liberation of Paris,
August 26, 1944

**SCAN TO VIEW THE
INTERACTIVE MAP**

INTERACTION EXERCISE

The journey of the Jewish people who rose from the ashes of the Holocaust, rebuilt their lives, and even established a homeland in Israel is a powerful testament to the resilience of the Jewish spirit, as well as a clarion call to the world declaring that the Word of God is true, for God Himself has not allowed the Jewish people to cease from being a nation before Him.

CREATE:

Imagine it's 1946 and you are having a conversation with a few Holocaust survivors. During the war, they were imprisoned in the Bergen-Belsen concentration camp. Now the war is over, but these survivors have no documents, no identification, and find themselves in a newly established displacement camp. What do you want to ask them? What do you think would've sustained them?

DISCUSS:

» What was the role of faith in sustaining life for the Jewish people after the Holocaust?

» What is inspirational to you about stories of resistance and survival and perseverance after the war? What breaks your heart?

INTERACTIVE MAP:

Use a **map** of post-war Europe and the Middle East to trace the routes of Jewish refugees to Israel. What hardships did they face? What level of determination was required?

By learning about the Holocaust, we can step into the shoes of those who lived it as well. Consider how their struggles and perseverance inspire your faith and how you can support Israel today, whether through prayer, education, or action.

Association of Jewish Ex-Servicemen and Women organized a silent march against the resurgence of Nazism in London, 1960

ENGAGE FURTHER

Explore more about the struggles the Jewish people faced after WWII **through this video**. As you watch, reflect on the resilience and strength of the Jewish people as they rebuilt their lives and communities after unimaginable loss, and consider how hope and determination can shape the future, even in the face of adversity.

REFLECTION AND ACTION

The Nazi Reich, though powerful for a time, was ultimately completely wiped out, while the Jewish people remained and thrived. We must always remember that Israel is important to God. In Zechariah 2:8, we read, *"For this is what the LORD Almighty says: 'After the Glorious One has sent me against the nations that have plundered you — for whoever touches you touches the apple of his eye...'"* (NIV).

After WWII, the Jewish people still had an uphill battle. They had to endure continued antisemitism in Europe, immigration restrictions in countries around the world, and Arab opposition to a Jewish homeland. Yet against all odds, the Jewish people survived, thrived, and continue to work toward repairing the world today.

POST-WWII LIBERATION STRUGGLES

This video details the impossible situation that European Jews found themselves in after the Nazis were defeated. It became clear that a return to the Jewish homeland was the only solution for the millions who had been forced from their homes during the Holocaust.

SCAN TO WATCH, OR VISIT:
CUFI.org/holocaustcourse

Liberation of Paris, August 26, 1944

Life in Israel today is vibrant and thriving — a living testament to hope and resilience after the Holocaust

REFLECT:

» What are your takeaways when you consider what the Jewish people went through in the Holocaust?

» Life wasn't automatically easy for the Jews after WWII. Post-liberation struggles, pain, and suffering were still real. What do you think about that?

» How does the establishment of the State of Israel affirm God's promises in Scripture?

ACT:

» Take a few minutes and get away to a quiet spot. Open a journal and write out a prayer to God about your thoughts or feelings about the Holocaust.

» Consider sharing what you've learned with your community or church, encouraging others to understand or support Israel.

» What is one thing you can practically do in your life or community to combat antisemitism?

The post-WWII struggles of Holocaust survivors teach us that even in the aftermath of unimaginable darkness, hope and new life are possible. We are reminded that we can always choose life, even if we've endured pain and suffering. As we look forward, we can, through education, prayer, and action, be strengthened in our walk with God and commitment to stand with His Chosen People.

Glossary of Terms:

TIKKUN OLAM (תיקון עולם):
A deeply held Jewish concept that means "Repair the world." Tikkun Olam emphasizes the responsibility to seek justice, brotherly love, and ethical living in an effort to improve or heal the world.

NOTES

NOTES

"For this is what the LORD Almighty says: 'After the Glorious One has sent me against the nations that have plundered you — for whoever touches you touches the apple of his eye...'"

ZECHARIAH 2:8 (NIV)

CUFI'S
HOLOCAUST
COURSE

FROM DEVASTATION TO THE ESTABLISHMENT OF THE STATE OF ISRAEL

CHRISTIANS UNITED FOR ISRAEL

FROM DEVASTATION TO THE ESTABLISHMENT OF THE STATE OF ISRAEL

LEARNING OBJECTIVE

In this section, we will explore the journey of the Jewish people from the devastation of the Holocaust to the miraculous establishment of the State of Israel in May of 1948. It examines how unwavering faith and perseverance despite immense challenges fueled their return to their ancestral homeland, Israel, overcoming unimaginable odds and fulfilling God's promises.

The Palestine Post: State of Israel is born, May 1948

HISTORICAL OVERVIEW

Following centuries of exile, persecution, and survival, the Jewish people achieved what should have been impossible: the liberation of their indigenous homeland after 2,000 years of exile — in the same land, as the same people, speaking the same language, worshipping the same God.

And yet that is the story of the Jewish people. In AD 70, General Titus of Rome marched against Jerusalem with legions of Roman soldiers. They besieged the city, ultimately overtook it, and subsequently destroyed it. The Jewish people were flung to the far corners of the earth. Yet, for two millennia they kept their Jewish heritage, traditions, Law, and customs.

No matter where they lived, they maintained their identity as Jews. After the devastation of the Holocaust, a great miracle occurred with the reestablishment of the State of Israel. Even though the Jewish people had lived in dispersion for thousands of years, in the 20th century, they resettled their ancestral homeland, once again set Jerusalem as their eternal capital, and revived the Hebrew language as the lingua franca of the Jewish people in the land of Israel.

The prophet Isaiah wrote: *"Who has ever heard of such things? Who has ever seen things like this? Can a country be born in a day or a nation be brought forth in a moment? Yet no sooner is Zion in labor than she gives birth to her children"* (Isaiah 66:8, NIV) The establishment of the State of Israel in the historic and Biblical homeland of the Jews is a proclamation of the power of the enduring Word of God.

HOPE AND STRUGGLE

Throughout WWII, millions of Jews had perished, and those who survived bore the scars of war. Many were lone survivors of their families or former communities.

In the days after VE Day (Victory in Europe Day) and the surrender of the German army to the Allied forces in 1945, the Jewish people were liberated from concentration camps across Europe.

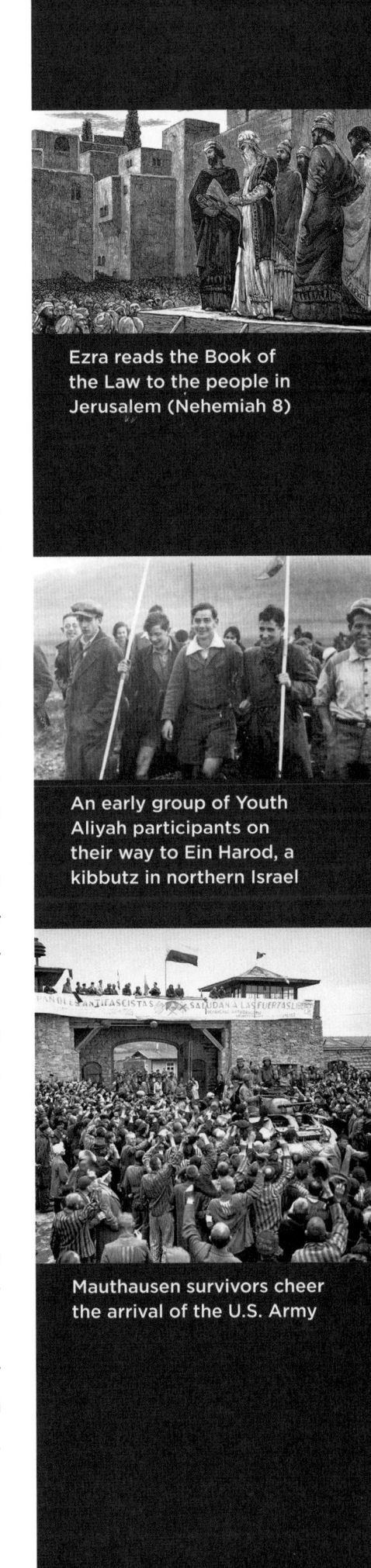

Ezra reads the Book of the Law to the people in Jerusalem (Nehemiah 8)

An early group of Youth Aliyah participants on their way to Ein Harod, a kibbutz in northern Israel

Mauthausen survivors cheer the arrival of the U.S. Army

Israel War of
Independence, 1948

Many would emigrate to Israel with the hope of setting up a Jewish homeland. But there was much work yet to be done.

Though the establishment of the State of Israel would be declared just three years after the war's end, it was still only a hope. In Israel, still known as Palestine as named by the Romans as an insult to the children of Israel, the British government oversaw the administration of the land. Jewish Holocaust survivors were often blocked from emigrating to Israel by British Navy vessels or stuck behind British-mandated blockades.

The British government hindered Jewish emigration to appease the Arab population, who were opposed to Jews returning home, and to uphold the restrictions outlined in the 1939 White Paper.

THE SHIP "THE EXODUS"

"The Exodus" after
British takeover, 1947

The ship "The Exodus" became one of the most profound symbols of the struggle for a Jewish homeland in Israel. While Jews were living in displaced persons camps and still stuck in Europe after WWII, they dreamed of emigrating to their ancestral and Biblical homeland.

The ship, the "President Warfield," was purchased and converted to hold as many passengers as possible. Over 4,500 Jewish refugees and Holocaust survivors boarded the ship and left the port of Sète, France. The ship flew a Honduran flag and left under cover of night.

However, news of the nature of the ship reached the British Navy, and an armada intercepted the ship. In an open sea ceremony, the passengers changed the name to "The Exodus" and prepared for boarding by British Marines.

Two British destroyers rammed the ship, and a battle broke out on the ship. The British won. The damaged ship was escorted to the port of Haifa, where the passengers were disembarked and set on three ships slated to leave immediately. They would not disembark in France, and the French government would not compel them. So,

The 50th anniversary medal
in honor of "The Exodus"

the British sent them to Hamburg, Germany, and, using clubs and hoses, forced them to disembark, and they were placed in camps, some former concentration camps.

Global outrage at the treatment of the Jews at the hands of the British reached newspapers worldwide and underscored the dire situation of Jewish refugees seeking a home.

DECLARATION OF THE STATE OF ISRAEL

Jewish provisional government in Tel Aviv to proclaim the new State of Israel

On May 14, 1948, the Jewish provisional government led by David Ben-Gurion declared the establishment of the State of Israel. Based on the acceptance of the 1947 United Nations Partition Plan as well as the official end of the British Mandate for Palestine, representatives assembled in Tel Aviv to proclaim the new State of Israel.

The United States was the first country to officially recognize Israel, and a message was sent by President Truman just 11 minutes after the declaration to the Jewish provisional government, recognizing it as the "de facto authority of the new State of Israel."

Jewish leadership had accepted the United Nations plan of two separate Jewish and Arab states; however, Arab rulers rejected it entirely. Though the nascent State of Israel extended peace toward

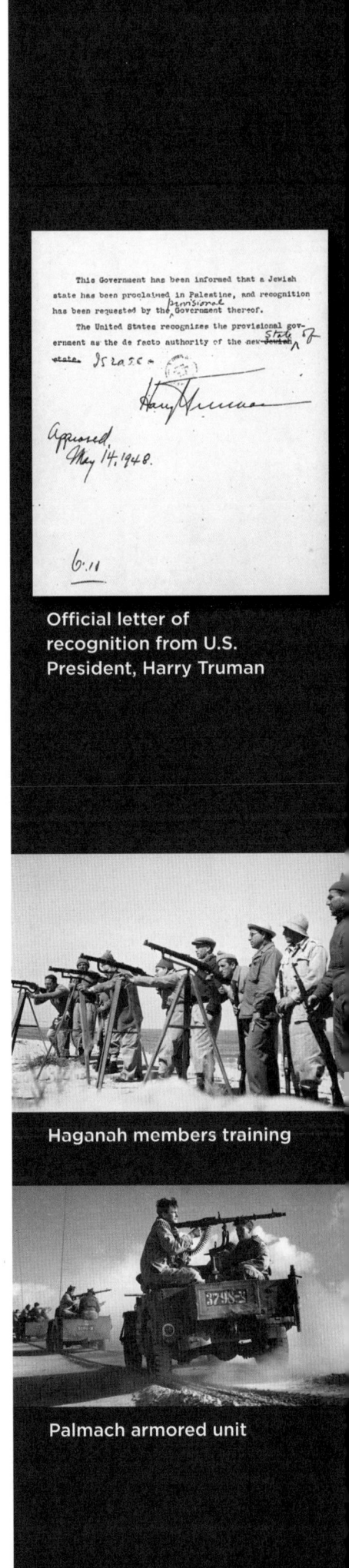

Official letter of recognition from U.S. President, Harry Truman

Haganah members training

Palmach armored unit

95

its Arab neighbors, within hours, five Arab nations — Jordan, Syria, Egypt, Lebanon, and Iraq — each attacked the fledgling country.

Israel's War of Independence would be the first of many wars between Israel and the Arab nations that surround it. Though Israel was outmatched and outgunned, the Jewish people's resilience to finally have a home on the earth, as well as the providential hand of God to bring the same to pass, saw Israel victorious.

In the end, Israel signed armistice agreements with the neighboring countries of Egypt, Jordan, Lebanon, and Syria and gained significant territory, even beyond the original borders as outlined by the United Nations Partition Plan. The new nation of Israel had recognizable borders, a formidable army, and a people resolutely united in their mission to rebuild the Jewish homeland promised to the descendants of Jacob.

TESTIMONIAL CONNECTION

The opening lines of the declaration of the establishment of the State of Israel read as follows:

> The Land of Israel was the birthplace of the Jewish people. Here their spiritual, religious and political identity was shaped. Here they first attained to statehood, created cultural values of national and universal significance and gave to the world the eternal Book of Books.

> After being forcibly exiled from their land, the people kept faith with it throughout their Dispersion and never ceased to pray and hope for their return to it and for the restoration in it of their political freedom.

> Impelled by this historic and traditional attachment, Jews strove in every successive generation to re-establish themselves in their ancient homeland. In recent decades they

Declaration of the establishment of the State of Israel

returned in their masses. Pioneers, defiant returnees, and defenders, they made deserts bloom, revived the Hebrew language, built villages and towns, and created a thriving community controlling its own economy and culture, loving peace but knowing how to defend itself, bringing the blessings of progress to all the country's inhabitants, and aspiring towards independent nationhood.

REFLECT:

» What stands out to you about the text?

» How do you think those in attendance felt on the evening of the proclamation?

KEY THEMES AND REFLECTION

The journey from the devastation of the Holocaust to the establishment of the State of Israel testifies to the enduring Covenant between God and the Jewish people and the fulfillment of His promises as seen throughout Scripture. In only three years, Holocaust survivors, still bearing the indelible marks of their suffering, came together to build a nation, secure their independence, and reclaim the land God promised to them.

God's Covenant with the Jewish People

The establishment of the State of Israel reflects the enduring faithfulness of God to His Covenant with the Jewish people. His promises, expressed through the words of Scripture, affirm His compassion, restoration, and unwavering commitment to His Chosen People. Viewing Israel and the Jewish people through this covenantal reality helps us recognize how divine providence shapes history, even in the face of impossible odds.

Front page of *The New York Times* at Independence Hall in Tel Aviv, Israel

Cheering and waving Israeli flags on Independence Day, Tel Aviv, May 14, 1948

A post office and a bank on a peaceful street in Jerusalem, 1950

Jews dancing at Kibbutz Gan Shmuel in Israel, marking "Chag HaBikkurim," the Festival of First Fruits, 1959

Parade of the Israel Defense Forces in 1960, Haifa

Menorah Garden, Jerusalem, Israel, circa 1960

» "...the LORD your God will bring you back from captivity, and have compassion on you, and gather you again from all the nations where the LORD your God has scattered you. If any of you are driven out to the farthest parts under heaven, from there the LORD your God will gather you, and from there He will bring you. Then the LORD your God will bring you to the land which your fathers possessed, and you shall possess it. He will prosper you and multiply you more than your fathers."
DEUTERONOMY 30:3-5 (NKJV)

» "Thus says the LORD of hosts: 'Behold, I will save My people from the land of the east and from the land of the west; I will bring them back, and they shall dwell in the midst of Jerusalem. They shall be My people and I will be their God, in truth and righteousness.'"
ZECHARIAH 8:7-8 (NKJV)

» "For I will take you from among the nations, gather you out of all countries, and bring you into your own land."
EZEKIEL 36:24 (NKJV)

» "I will bring back the captives of My people Israel; they shall build the waste cities and inhabit them; they shall plant vineyards and drink wine from them; they shall also make gardens and eat fruit from them. I will plant them in their land, and no longer shall they be pulled up from the land I have given them," says the LORD your God.
AMOS 9:14-15 (NKJV)

The Power of Hope

The Jewish people's journey from being prisoners in concentration camps to establishing their own home in their own land took extraordinary courage, determination, and hope. Many survivors of the war had nowhere else to go, no family left, and no country to turn to for help.

They clung to hope. They decided that it was finally time to do everything possible to establish a home for the Jews in the world. The hope for a Jewish homeland would no longer just be rumors but a real place with real borders and even their own language.

For 2,000 years, the longing for the return to Zion had become deeply rooted in the Jewish experience. For two millennia, the Jewish people were marginalized, chased away, persecuted, and slaughtered all over the world.

The Zionist vision to have a sovereign Jewish state in the land of Israel was a dream. Finally, in 1948, even though they were compelled to immediately go to war in defense of their freedom, the dream became reality.

The creation of Israel in 1948 was not just a political achievement but the culmination of thousands of years of hope as well. In the Diaspora, hope kept Jewish communities united. Hope helped create a space for the dream of independence to one day come to pass.

To this day, the State of Israel shines as a symbol and a beacon of the power of hope to the world, physical proof that the miraculous is possible.

REFLECT:

» What comes to mind when you read God's promises in Scripture to bring the Jewish people back to the land of Israel?

» How has the power of hope shaped life for the Jewish people throughout history?

INTERACTION EXERCISE

When we engage with history, it becomes more alive in our hearts and minds. On May 14, 1948, representatives of the Jewish Provisional Government met in Tel Aviv. Under the banner of Theodor Herzl, they marked a day that would forever live in history.

Yom Ha'atzmaut (Israel Independence Day) parade in Jerusalem, 1960

Western Wall, Jerusalem, Israel

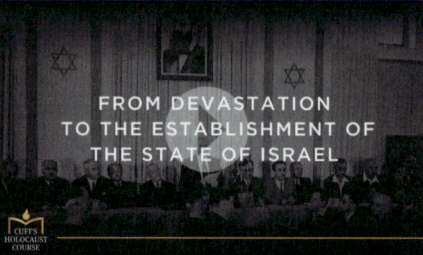

FROM DEVASTATION
TO THE ESTABLISHMENT OF
THE STATE OF ISRAEL

In this video, learn about the antisemitism, persecution, and attacks the Jewish people have endured since Israel became a sovereign nation in 1948.

SCAN TO WATCH, OR VISIT:
CUFI.org/holocaustcourse

Imagine May 14, 1948:

Imagine you are Jewish, you are living in 1948, and you just survived the Holocaust. You have a tattooed number on your forearm from time in a concentration camp in Poland, but in the last three years since WWII ended, you have been able to make Aliyah to the land of Israel.

You don't know what the future holds for you, for the Jewish people as a whole, or for what will become a new country once again called Israel.

Tonight, you are in Tel Aviv, and it is May 14, 1948. You are outside the Tel Aviv Museum with a crowd of people, and David Ben-Gurion has just declared the establishment and the independence of the State of Israel.

DISCUSS:

A powerful mixture of hope and excitement filled the streets of Tel Aviv that night. For Jewish people in Israel and across the globe, life would never be the same. Finally, they had a country of their own.

» What is the feeling in the air?
» What are the people in the crowd saying all around you?
» What emotions do you feel coursing through you?

ENGAGE FURTHER

The journey of the Jewish people is marked by resilience and profound hope. **Watch this video** to explore the ongoing challenges they faced in the wake of WWII and the aftermath of the Holocaust, leading to the rebirth of the State of Israel.

REFLECTION AND ACTION

The journey from the devastation of the Holocaust to the establishment of the State of Israel is a story that can only be understood within the framework of the supernatural. David Ben-Gurion once said, "In Israel, in order to be a realist you must believe in miracles."

Against all odds, the Jewish people rose up from the ashes of the Holocaust and began to make a beautiful country in the land of Israel. The Holocaust was one of the darkest periods of time in all of human history. It brought to the fore with glaring clarity the need for a home for the Jewish people.

A PORTION OF ISRAEL'S DECLARATION OF INDEPENDENCE READS:

"The catastrophe which recently befell the Jewish people — the massacre of millions of Jews in Europe — was another clear demonstration of the urgency of solving the problem of its homelessness by re-establishing in Eretz-Israel the Jewish State, which would open the gates of the homeland wide to every Jew and confer upon the Jewish people the status of a fully privileged member of the community of nations."

In the wake of the Holocaust, the miracle of the founding of Israel is a clear sign to Christians around the world that the Word of God is true. Additionally, it highlights the need for Christians to rise up and stand in support of Israel and the Jewish people.

INITIATE:

The modern State of Israel carries with it enormous historical and Biblical significance. To bless Israel, to support Israel, and to stand with Israel are gifts given to every Christian around the world.

David Ben-Gurion, first Prime Minister of Israel

Old City, Jerusalem, Israel

Ancient olive trees in the Garden of Gethsemane, nestled at the foot of the Mount of Olives in Jerusalem

>> Take out a pen and paper and find a quiet spot. Consider what you have learned through this course. Think about the stories you've read or the lessons you've learned.

>> Spend time in prayer. As you do, set every other concern and thought aside for a few moments and commit to focusing your prayer time on praying for Israel and the Jewish people.

>> Ask God what He wants you to do.

Street of Jerusalem, Old City Alley, made with hand-carved stones

The weight of the birth of Israel in our time can never be fully comprehended. It is truly a miracle. By supporting Israel and standing with the Jewish people, we align ourselves with God's Word and come into the blessing of those who choose to bless the descendants of Abraham, Isaac, and Jacob. Those who bless God's people, Israel:

"I will make you a great nation; I will bless you and make your name great; and you shall be a blessing. I will bless those who bless you, and I will curse him who curses you; and in you all the families of the earth shall be blessed."

GENESIS 12:2-3 (NKJV)

Glossary of Terms:

1947 UNITED NATIONS PARTITION PLAN:
A plan to divide the British Mandate for Palestine into separate Jewish and Arab states, with Jerusalem as an international city under UN administration. The plan was accepted by Jewish leadership and rejected by Arab leadership.

DAVID BEN-GURION:
The first Prime Minister of the State of Israel, a central figure in the founding of the nation, and leader in the Zionist movement. He was a visionary leader of the Jewish people and declared Israel's independence in 1948, as well as guiding the young nation through its formative years, including the War of Independence.

HAGANAH:
A Jewish paramilitary organization established in 1920 as an underground defense force to protect Jewish communities in Mandatory Palestine. It began as a militia and eventually evolved into an organized military, laying the groundwork for what would become the Israel Defense Forces (IDF).

ISRAEL WAR OF INDEPENDENCE (1948):
An attack waged on Israel within hours of her declared independence. Five regular Arab armies attacked with overwhelming superiority both in number and equipment including armor, artillery, and air power. However, Israel won the war and gained significant territory and land.

PALMACH:
An elite military unit within the Haganah, established in 1941. The Palmach played a critical role in defending Jewish communities as well as military operations against British rule and Arab opposition.

NOTES

"It's not a matter of maintaining the status quo. We have to create a dynamic state, oriented towards expansion."

DAVID BEN-GURION

CALL TO ACTION

Bearing witness to the Holocaust through stories and photographs leaves an indelible mark on the soul. The names of those who perished and the lost potential of their stolen lives must always be remembered.

Knowledge of the Holocaust must lead to action as well. For if there is no action, then the possibility of history repeating itself increases exponentially. We cannot forget. We must not. The light of the candle of remembrance must never be extinguished.

The Holocaust teaches us the depths of hatred and prejudice and fear and anger to which mankind can stoop. It shows us what is possible in the hearts of men and on the face of the earth if evil is left unchecked. And we also learn of the power of the human spirit, of the strength of hope, and of what is possible when men and women lean into courage and stand against darkness.

REMEMBRANCE IS SACRED

One of the most important aspects in the Jewish tradition is to remember. Within Jewish life, to remember is not a passive act; rather, it is an active call and deeply embedded in Jewish thought with roots in the Torah.

In Exodus 20:8, God said, *"Remember the Sabbath day, to keep it holy"* (NASB). And again in Deuteronomy 5:15, He said, *"And remember that you were a slave in the land of Egypt, and the LORD your God brought you out from there by a mighty hand and by an outstretched arm; therefore the LORD your God commanded you to keep the Sabbath day"* (NKJV). For thousands of years, the Jewish people have indeed remembered the words of the Lord.

For the millions of Jewish men, women, and children who were murdered by the Nazis, to remember their names and stories is to honor them, in blessed memory. It is vital that the passing of time be kept from relegating their existence on this earth to mere history; what they endured must never be forgotten.

To that end, every year, there is a day set aside in Israel called Yom HaShoah. This sacred day was established by the Israeli government in 1953 to commemorate the six million Jews who lost their lives. It is also a day to remember the heroism and resistance of countless brave souls who fought back.

The date of Yom HaShoah falls on the 27th of Nisan on the Hebrew calendar, correlating with the Warsaw Ghetto Uprising, which began on April 19, 1943. On the Gregorian calendar, the date correlates to a day in either April or May.

When a Jew passes away today or falls in battle while defending Israel, it is customary to say, "May their memory be a blessing." In Jewish tradition, remembrance is more than an act; it's a core element of identity, intertwining the past and present to preserve the future.

PRAYER FOR ISRAEL

Prayer is central to the lives of Jews and Christians — a sacred dialogue with God, seeking His guidance and abiding in His presence. An incredible fact is that we have an exhortation within Holy Scripture to pray for a specific city upon the face of the earth.

Plaque in the Garden Tomb, Jerusalem, Israel

Psalm 122:6–9 says, *"Pray for the peace of Jerusalem: 'May they prosper who love you. Peace be within your walls, prosperity within your palaces.' For the sake of my brethren and companions, I will now say, 'Peace be within you.' Because of the house of the LORD our God I will seek your good"* (NKJV). It is a call for believers to pray for the peace of Jerusalem.

Moreover, Isaiah wrote, *"For Zion's sake I will not keep silent, for Jerusalem's sake I will not remain quiet, till her vindication shines out like the dawn, her salvation like a blazing torch"* (Isaiah 62:1, NIV). Zion is a name for Jerusalem, and through the prophet's words, we are exhorted to intercede on behalf of Jerusalem.

Jerusalem is mentioned throughout Scripture and is special upon the earth to God. It is the City of David (2 Samuel 5:7) and the City of the Great King (Psalm 48:2). God chose Jerusalem to set His name there (2 Chronicles 6:6); it is His chosen dwelling (Psalm 132:13), and His eyes and heart will be there forever (2 Chronicles 7:16).

Jerusalem is the eternal capital of Israel (1 Kings 11:36), the inheritance of the Jewish people (Amos 9:15), and the future fulfillment of the plans of God (Zechariah 12:1–9). Jerusalem cannot be separated from the Jewish people. To pray for the peace of Jerusalem is to pray for the peace of Israel and the good of the Jewish people.

Each moment dedicated in prayer for Israel and the Jewish people is time well spent. May we be those who fill the halls of Heaven with our prayers and intercession on behalf of God's Chosen People and the land He loves.

CHRISTIAN ACTION

For Christians, it is a righteous obligation to remember the Holocaust, to stand with the Jewish people, and to combat antisemitism.

Millions of Jews died in Europe under the most horrible conditions. Let us stand with the Jewish people today. Let "Never Again" be more than a declaration; let it inspire courage, decisive action, and meaningful advocacy for lasting change.

Isaiah wrote, *"But you, Israel, are My servant, Jacob whom I have chosen, the descendants of Abraham My friend. You whom I have taken from the ends of the earth, and called from its farthest regions, and said to you, 'You are My servant, I have chosen you and have not cast you away...'"* (Isaiah 41:8–9, NKJV). God Himself has declared that He has chosen Israel. He will never cast them aside.

We must commit to resolutely stand with Israel and the Jewish people. History has shown that the world will never stop trying to attack them, but may we work to ensure that their light endures for countless future generations. Choose today which side of history you will stand on: Will you stand with Israel, or will you remain silent?

GET INVOLVED WITH CUFI

ATTEND A CUFI EVENT

Learn the facts you need to defend and support Israel. We hold over 50 events across the U.S. each month. When a CUFI event comes to your city, church, or campus, please join us and bring your friends. **CUFI.org/event**

FOLLOW US ON SOCIAL MEDIA

Follow us on Facebook, Twitter, Instagram, YouTube, TikTok, and LinkedIn for breaking news and engaging educational content. We share Israel's story in real-time with millions of Christians across multiple platforms.

- @ChristiansUnitedforIsrael
- @CUFI
- ChristiansUnitedforIsrael
- OfficialCUFI
- @CUFIOfficial
- Christians United for Israel

SIGN THE ISRAEL PLEDGE

Every signature demonstrates Christians are committed to Israel's security. Every signature makes Israel safer. **CUFI.org/pledge**

BRING CUFI TO YOUR COMMUNITY

Educate your community by bringing a CUFI speaker to your city. CUFI speakers provide dynamic presentations that will open your community's eyes to the current situation in the Middle East and why and how they should stand with Israel. **CUFI.org/host**

ATTEND SUMMIT IN WASHINGTON, D.C

Join thousands of pro-Israel Christians in our nation's capital at our premier annual event to stand up and speak up for Israel and the Jewish people. CUFI members learn from national and international leaders and visit Capitol Hill to encourage every member of Congress to support policies that strengthen the U.S.–Israel relationship. **CUFI.org/summit**

SIGN THE SHINE THE LIGHT PLEDGE

As members of CUFI, we will not simply curse the darkness; we are committed to shining the light on antisemitism in all its forms, wherever it may be found. Please join us in pledging to Shine the Light and commit to combatting this scourge. Pledge to Shine the Light at **CUFI.org/shinepledge**

SUPPORT CUFI'S FILM ON ANTISEMITISM

CUFI's full-length documentary *Never Again?* is a one-of-a-kind film that features the journeys of two men—late Holocaust survivor Irving Roth and transformed radical anti-Israel activist Kasim Hafeez. The film follows them throughout Slovakia, Poland, the United Kingdom, Israel, and the U.S. Their personal accounts vividly depict the parallels between the hatred of Jews preceding the Holocaust, which culminated in the slaughter of six million Jews, and today's widespread antisemitism. **neveragainthemovie.com**

HOST A SMALL GROUP STUDY

CUFI's small group curriculum using CUFI's *The Israel Course* enables our members to gather together and learn about Israel. **CUFI.org/group**

JOIN CUFI'S COFFEE BREAK

Learn about Israel's history, political situation, and Biblical significance in minutes. Each week, you will receive a bite-sized—yet powerful—Israel lesson in your inbox. **CUFI.org/coffee-break**

CUFI DAILY BRIEFING

CUFI provides a daily briefing via email to keep you up-to-date on the latest Israel and Middle East news. Monday through Friday, you will receive in your inbox a snapshot of current events surrounding Israel. Sign up to receive CUFI's Daily Briefing to ensure you never miss an important development. **CUFI.org/daily-briefing**

CUFI ON CAMPUS

CUFI on Campus equips Christian students from across the country with Biblical principles and knowledge of the Middle East to be effective voices for Israel on their college campuses. To date, CUFI on Campus has trained over 4,200 students, has a presence on over 230 campuses throughout the United States, and has taken more than 700 students to Israel. **CUFIoncampus.org**

CUFI HIGH SCHOOL

CUFI High School educates high school student leaders to prepare them to combat antisemitism and stand up for Israel in their high schools and on their future college campuses. **CUFIhighschool.org**

DAUGHTERS FOR ZION PRAYER NETWORK

DFZ is an initiative of Christians United for Israel whose purpose is to organize intercessory prayer groups in America to pray for the peace of Jerusalem, the well-being of the State of Israel and her people, the growth and development of Christians United for Israel, and specific prayer alerts that arise through the year. To date, Daughters for Zion has thousands of members throughout the U.S. and the world. **daughtersforzion.org**

THE ISRAEL COLLECTIVE

The Israel Collective (IC), a national initiative of Christians United for Israel, has taken 1,000 millennial influencers to Israel. The IC communicates the truth about Israel and the Middle East to the next generation through social media and films that highlight the heart and the people of Israel. **Israelcollective.org**

THE ISRAEL COURSE

In 20 in-depth lessons, learn why Christians should support Israel. Delve into Israel's Biblical, historical, and geopolitical significance with videos, quizzes, journal prompts, and more. Enroll today and be the best defender of Israel you can be. **CUFI.org/course**

Endnotes:

1   Dawidowicz, Lucy S. *The War Against the Jews, 1933–1945*. New York: Bantam Books, 1975, p. 44–45

2   Dawidowicz, *The War Against the Jews*, p. 44

3   N/A. "This Map Shows Many of the Synagogues Destroyed on Kristallnacht." My Jewish Learning. N/D. Web. https://www.myjewishlearning.com/article/this-map-shows-many-of-the-synagogues-destroyed-on-kristallnacht/

4   N/A. "Germans pass by the broken shop window of a Jewish-owned business that was destroyed during Kristallnacht." United States Holocaust Memorial Museum. November 10, 1938. Web. https://collections.ushmm.org/search/catalog/pa16792

5   Levin, Talia. "Kristallnacht: The light extinguished 83 years ago still burns bright." The Jerusalem Post. 2021. Web. https://www.jpost.com/diaspora/antisemitism/kristallnacht-the-light-extinguished-83-years-ago-still-burns-bright-684690

6   Langer, Klaus. "Klaus Langer's Diary Entry on Kristallnacht, November 11, 1938." Facing History & Ourselves. Updated August 2, 2016. Web. https://www.facinghistory.org/resource-library/klaus-langers-diary-entry-kristallnacht-november-11-1938

7   Dawsey, Jason. "Kristallnacht: The Night of Broken Glass." The National WWII Museum: New Orleans. December 1, 2023. Web. https://www.nationalww2museum.org/war/articles/kristallnacht-night-broken-glass

8   Lasker-Wallfisch, Anita. "Anita Lasker-Wallfisch MBE." Holocaust Memorial Day Trust. 2003. Web. https://hmd.org.uk/resource/anita-lasker-wallfisch/

9   Wiesel, Elie. *Night*. trans. Marion Wiesel. New York: Hill and Wang, 2006, p. 34

CHRISTIANS UNITED FOR ISRAEL
PO Box 1307 | San Antonio, TX 78295
info@cufi.org | 210-477-4714